The
STEPS
Story

GW00374511

Also available:

*The B*WITCHED Story* by Pippa Richardson

Teresa Maughan

BOXTREE

First published 1999 by Boxtree
an imprint of Macmillan Publishers Ltd
25 Eccleston Place London SW1W 9NF
Basingstoke and Oxford

www.macmillan.co.uk

Associated companies throughout the world

ISBN 0 7522 1823 9

1 3 5 7 9 8 6 4 2

A CIP catalogue record for this book is available from the British Library.

Typeset by SX Composing DTP, Rayleigh, Essex
Printed by Mackays of Chatham PLC, Chatham, Kent

Contents

INTRODUCTION

Pop's happiest group has to be Steps. Smiley, sunny and sexy – that's Lisa, Faye, Claire, H and Lee. The cheeksters of pop love having a laugh, and that shines through in their upbeat music. Whack on a Steps track and you'll be dancing yourself dizzy well into the night – whether you want to or not – 'cos these guys are simply irresistible. Who'd have thought that this decade's biggest music'n'dance sensation were struggling to get their talents noticed just a couple of years ago. All five Steps were living a normal humdrum existence just dreaming about a life of fame and fortune doing what they do best – singing and dancing!!

And that's what's so fab about 'the Abba of the 1990s' as they've been described by numerous pop pundits – they are so approachable. Lisa, Faye, Claire, H and Lee really are the girls and boys next door! Steps have played anywhere and everywhere in a bid to get noticed, and from shopping mall to TV studio these five good-looking young laydees and gentlemen inspired everyone who saw them. It didn't matter if you were male or female. Boys could pretend to be H or Lee, while girls could aim at being the next Faye, Lisa or Claire. And when it came to fanciable fodder, you simply reverse the roles!

When Steps came on the pop scene, they brought a new dance for every hit single. And when they stepped out on tour they had a stage act that was every bit as entertaining as a panto, with plenty of audience participation. Oh no it wasn't, oh yes it was! The show was as action-packed as the Disney cartoons which have provided the inspiration for a Steps medley. Dancing, singing, dressing up . . . everything that kids of all ages love to do in a world of make-believe. But for Steps the fantasy became reality when their first album *Step One* shot through the million mark (*The Times* newspaper made it their album of the year) – a new force in pop had arrived.

Ask Steps the secret of their success and (if they've got a spare moment) they'll tell you it's all down to hard work. All five have slogged their way up the showbiz ladder through cabaret, failed groups and holiday camps, and no way were they going to let their golden chance slip by. As Steps-mania has taken a worldwide hold, their passports have picked up ever more exotic stamps as they've jetted across the globe in a vain attempt to satisfy demand.

Now with this book, the most comprehensive on the group so far, you can chart Steps' progress from the five hopefuls who answered an advert to the fully-fledged superstars they are today. There's no doubt their star will continue to rise, and the autumn 1999 release of their second album – 'Not to be called *Step Two*,' they insist – will give them another platinum disc for their wall, and doubtless another shoal of hit singles to entertain us.

The blueprint for Steps' success mixes music, image, energy and imagination in equal measure. It's one that's successfully crossed national boundaries and language barriers (a Malaysian has actually done a cover of '5,6,7,8' in Mandarin!) and looks set to continue to do so. The facts and figures stuffed between these covers tell part of the story . . . their music will do the rest. So switch on the stereo, and get reading.

STEPS PROFILES

LISA

Name

Lisa Scott-Lee

Nickname

Party Steps

Birthday

5 November

Astrological sign

Scorpio

Family

Mum Jan, Dad Tony, brothers Stephen, Andy and Anthony

Height

5 feet 3 inches

Colour of hair

Reddish brown

Colour of eyes

Green

Distinguishing feature

A birthmark shaped like a water stain on her stomach

Hobbies

Art

Childhood ambition

To be an astronaut

Favourite film

'*The Three Amigos* with Dan Ackroyd 'cos it's so funny and I loved *The Lost Boys*, too.'

Favourite actor

'Claire Danes and I'm a big Will Smith fan.'

Favourite singer

Robbie Williams

Favourite band

Texas

Favourite sport

Snooker

Likes to eat

Crab sticks

Best comfort food

A cup of tea and a packet of chocolate digestives

Likes to wear

Trainers with big soles

Best quality

'I'm outgoing and confident. If you've got a bit of confidence you can go far in life.'

Worst quality

'I'm incredibly stubborn and can cut off my nose to spite my face.'

Any regrets?

'I only have one 'cos I don't really believe in regrets – but I wish I hadn't given up the piano. I was going through my grades and getting really good, but I started singing and dancing and just didn't have the time. I'm going to take it up again soon, though.'

Most hated body part

'My feet – they're dancer's feet and they're yucky!'

First snog

'It was behind the school hall with a boy called Stephen when I was eleven.'

Love is . . .

'Only wanting to be with that one special person.'

Hero

'My Grandad.'

Favourite TV shows

'EastEnders, Corrie, Emmerdale, Brookside! I love the soaps, but I can't keep up with them these days, which is a shame.'

Catchphrase

Minger! (Horrible!)

Secret

'I like being kissed on my neck. It's quite a sensitive area, but no hickies!'

Would most like to play in a movie . . .

Baby in *Dirty Dancing*

Favourite country visited with Steps

Australia – 'I'd like to live there when I'm grown-up.'

Decided to be famous when?

'The day I was born!'

Would most like to forget . . .

'We got very silly with a photocopier in Germany and I ended up photo-copying my bottom.'

Pre-fame jobs

Worked in McDonald's and a bakery

Biggest fear

'Being burnt – I'd absolutely hate to be caught in a fire. Actually, we saw a really bad fire when we were in Spain. As we came out of the hotel we were engulfed by all this smoke. It was the start of a massive fire and ended up with this huge block of flats being burned down – it was awful.'

'Lisa just walks into a room and blokes just stare. it's this weird, magnetic, unexplained thing – blokes cannot help looking at her.' Faye

'Lisa goes cross-eyed when she sees a magpie, so it looks like she's seeing two. She's so superstitious she makes up her own rules!' Lee

'We all went to the cinema together in Scotland to see *Scream 2* and we must have been the loudest people in there. Lisa was squealing and going "oooooh . . . ahhhh!" all the way through and we were giggling . . .' Lee

H

Name

Ian Watkins

Nickname

H (for Hyperactive Steps)

Birthday

8 May

Astrological sign

Taurus

Family

Mum, Dad, brothers Jamie and Alyn

Colour of hair

Blond

Colour of eyes

Blue (but sometimes wears coloured contact lenses)

Height

5 feet 8 inches

Favourite sport

Swimming

Hobby
Eating
Childhood ambition
Gardener
Favourite film
'*The Muppets Take Manhattan* and the Roald Dahl film *Witches*. I like all the old musicals too, like *Annie* and *Oliver* . . .'
Favourite actor
'I like Meryl Streep and Glenn Close. And I like Leo DiCaprio, but then, who doesn't?'
Favourite bands
The Corrs, Backstreet Boys
Favourite singer
Janet Jackson
Likes to eat
'Pizza, burgers . . . anything and everything!'
Best comfort food
'Popcorn, chocolate and cheese and chive Pringles.'
Likes to wear
Jeans, mostly
Best qualities
'I don't pretend to be anything I'm not. Lots of people try to be really cool when they're not – I know I'm not cool. I just like to have a laugh.'
Worst quality
'I'm annoying. I don't know when to stop.'
Most hated body part
'I'm too skinny!'
First snog
'I was about twelve and I took a girl in my class to the pictures.'
Love is . . .
'Fantastic!'

Hero

Best mate Billie

Fave clothes

Jeans

Catchphrase

'Fab!'

Secret

'I'd like to buy a castle this year. It'll have a big moat and I'll invite all my friends round for parties.'

Would most like to play in a movie . . .

'The little boy in *The Navigator* (played by Ethan Hawke).'

Favourite country

'Singapore and Taiwan – they're amazing for shopping!'

Decided to be famous when?

'I used to dance in front of the mirror and dream about being famous.'

Earliest memory

'I was ill when I was five and my mum gave me Night Nurse. I wouldn't swallow it so she held my nose to make it go down. It was horrible!'

Pre-fame jobs

Clothes assistant, car valeter and Redcoat at a holiday camp

Would like to be remembered as . . .

'Genuine, fun, a good friend . . . Actually, I'd like to be remembered, full stop! Not to be remembered would be awful . . .'

'H makes me laugh a lot because he's always messing about. He covered me in banana leaves and wrapped me up in toilet paper – like a mummy – in one hotel. I just stood there having a giggling fit!' Claire

'If you want everyone to know something tell H a secret and he'll end up telling the whole world!' Lisa

'H is a terrible liar. If you want to keep something secret, he pulls this daft face and makes it obvious we're not telling the truth.' Faye

'H is such a great person and lovely to be around, but when you're round a lovely person twenty-four hours a day even they can get on your nerves!' Lisa

FAYE

Name
Faye Tozer
Nickname
Curly, Smiley Steps
Birthday
14 November
Astrological sign
Scorpio
Family
Mum, Dad, sister Claire
Colour of hair
Blonde
Colour of eyes
Blue
Height
5 feet 7 inches
Hobbies
Clubbing, walking, watching TV
Favourite sport
Trampolining
Favourite film
'*The Fifth Element*. It was so full of action and I really like Bruce Willis.'

Favourite actor

'Will "Fresh Prince" Smith and I'm really into Cameron Diaz after *There's Something About Mary*.'

Favourite band

All Saints

Favourite singer

Madonna, Janet Jackson, Mick Hucknall

Childhood ambition

To become a sculptor

Likes to eat

Crisps (Pringles for preference)

Best comfort food

Hawaiian pizza and cake!

Likes to wear

Space trousers

Best quality

'I'm very ambitious. If I want something I'll really go for it and put all my energy into getting whatever it is.'

Worst quality

'I'm not always as confident as I need to be and I miss opportunities.'

Most hated body part

'My ears – they stick out too much!'

Love is . . .

'What makes the world go round.'

Hero

Madonna

Fave clothes

Space trousers

Catchphrase

'Lush'

Most like to play in a movie . . .

'Jodie Foster in *Contact* – a very dramatic, brave woman.'

Decided to be famous when?

'I think I was about six.'

Dislikes

'Wrists and necks 'cos I'm so squeamish. It's all blood related . . . Tight necklaces around the neck . . . This morning a girl on the telly was wearing a necklace that was just a bit too tight. I had to switch it off 'cos it was making me all hot and flushed.'

Earliest memory

'When I was about three and I was ill in bed. My mum was scraping paint off the wall so she could redecorate. The sun was shining. It's a really warm, happy memory.'

Pre-fame jobs

Cooking pizza at Whipsnade Zoo.

'Claire and Faye are really superstitious and say things like "Don't step on that line, don't walk under there," and so on. I think it's stupid – I walk under ladders on purpose just to prove a point!' Lisa

'When you get Faye talking, you just can't shut her up. She just keeps going and going. You try to get a word in but she'll carry on, and you're like, "Take a breath, take a breath!"' Lee

'I get jealous that Faye and Claire have nicer outfits than I have, that always winds me up!' Lisa

LEE

Name

Lee Latchford Evans

Nickname
Latch, Sensible Steps
Birthday
28 January
Astrological sign
Aquarius
Family
Mum Stella, Dad Billy, sister Carly
Colour of hair
Dark brown
Colour of eyes
Hazel/green
Height
'5 feet 9½ inches (don't forget the half!)'
Hobbies
Watching videos, playing computer games, martial arts
Childhood ambition
'Always acting!'
Favourite film
'My favourite film of all time is called *Some Kind Of Wonderful*.'
Favourite actor
'Mel Gibson is my all-time fave, and at the moment I like Neve Campbell.'
Favourite band
Backstreet Boys
Favourite singers
Louise, Robbie Williams
Likes to eat
'Pizza, pizza and more pizza!'
Best comfort food
Doritos
Likes to wear
Levi's

Best quality

'A sense of humour. Then you can let things pass you by and not get you down . . .'

Worst quality

'I'm caring – sometimes too caring. It works both ways and sometimes people are like, "Just leave me alone!"'

Most hated body part

'My legs – they're horrid!'

First snog

'My first snog was when I was about six.'

Love is . . .

'Happiness. It's a very special feeling!'

Hero

Robbie Williams

Fave clothes

Jeans

Catchphrase

'Cool'

Secret

'I love being kissed all over!'

Most like to play in a movie . . .

'*Star Wars*' Han Solo, 'cos he's a bit of a rebel.'

Decided to be famous when?

'I never decided but I always felt that I would be. I remember saying that I'd leave my mark on the world before I died. I think I've started the right way.'

Favourite country visited with Steps

'Singapore because it's very clean and tidy, each tree looks like it's pruned to perfection.'

Pre-fame jobs

Paperboy, milkman, barman and shop assistant

'Lee is the most serious member of the band, and the

rest of Steps will tell you exactly the same thing.' Lisa

'Lee laughs at his own jokes – or if he knows something no one else does he starts grinning.' Lisa

'Lee is very trustworthy so you know he'll keep a secret.' Claire

CLAIRE

Name
Claire Richards
Nickname
Claire Bear, Clarabell, Gadget Steps
Birthday
17 September
Astrological sign
Virgo
Family
Mum, Dad, sister Gemma
Colour of hair
Blonde
Colour of eyes
Light green
Height
5 feet 6 inches
Distinguishing feature
A birthmark on her left arm that is visible after she's been sunbathing
Hobbies
Singing, reading, hanging out with friends
Childhood ambition
To be a chef
Favourite film
'One of the funniest films I've seen was *Liar Liar* with Jim Carrey.'

Favourite actor

Leo DiCaprio, Michelle Pfeiffer and George Clooney

Favourite singers

Celine Dion, Karen Carpenter

Favourite band

Backstreet Boys

Favourite sport

Football

Likes to eat

Ice cream

Best comfort food

Ice cream, popcorn, pizza and nachos with cheese

Likes to wear

Combat trousers

Best quality

'I'm pretty laid-back and very loyal.'

Worst quality

'Sometimes I'm too easy-going which goes against you because people take advantage . . . I think I'm a bit too generous – I can't stop buying presents for other people. I get really carried away and it's like a real buzz when I'm buying stuff. I have to stop it 'cos I've never got any money!'

Most hated body part

'My bum, my thighs, my legs, my nose . . .'

Worst snog

'When I was twelve and on holiday in the Canary Islands. He had braces and it was really sloppy and gross!'

Love is . . .

'Oh, my God! I don't know!'

Hero

Karen Carpenter

Fave clothes

Combats and trainers

Catchphrase

'Fantastic!'

Secret

'My perfect bloke would be someone who's fun, good-looking, makes me laugh and, preferably, has lots of cash.'

Would most like to play in a movie . . .

Julia Roberts in *Pretty Woman*

Decided to be famous when?

'When I was in the womb! When I was a kid, I always used to say I was going to be rich and famous.'

Earliest memory

'When I got my first bike. It was a present from my uncle and he got up at the crack of dawn and ran to our house on Christmas morning just to see our happy faces.'

Pre-fame jobs

Greengrocer, florist, shop assistant, envelope stuffer and a steward at Wembley Arena

Would like to be remembered as . . .

'I'd like to think I was well-liked and that I'd achieved everything I'd set out to. I really don't want to have any regrets and I'd like to feel happy with everything I'd done.'

'We call her Intensive Claire because she's so accident-prone.' H

'We'll get ready in about fifteen minutes, then wait an hour for Claire. Then again, Lee is quite fussy . . .' H

'Claire's the Steps cook. All H can cook is tuna pasta with kidney beans, tuna pasta with sweetcorn, tuna pasta with mayo and tuna pasta with ketchup!' Lisa

STEPPING OUT

Some groups grow up together, while others like B*Witched and Cleopatra are friends and relations whose family ties keep them together in the choppy, storm-tossed seas of pop where so many hopefuls are bobbing, trying to avoid the icebergs. Then there are other kids who follow their parents up the slippery showbusiness ladder, like Crispan Mills, the blond-hairdo guitar god who fronts rock hopefuls Kula Shaker. His mum is 1960s starlet Hayley Mills, the Kate Winslet of her time, so stardom was nothing new to young Crispan.

Steps were complete newcomers when it came to the fame game. Like the Spice Girls and Five, to name but two, they came together at someone else's bidding. But having found each other, they suddenly discovered a kind of magic that illuminated everything they did. Call it star quality, call it what you want – it was clear that this was a group which added up to much more than the sum of its parts. All that the five would-be stars had in common was ambition, talent, good looks and a subscription to *The Stage*.

For those who've never seen it, perhaps we should explain that *The Stage* is more than just a magazine – it's the equivalent of a showbusiness job centre. You don't have to go and queue up to sign on, but just like the cards in the window with job descriptions on them you can find opportunities in this mag that might – just might – change your life. That's how it was when a guy called Tim Byrne decided to form a group. His track record had been in television, being the brains behind shows like *Dance Energy* and *The Word* (the big break for photogenic presenter Dani Behr), so he was very aware of the visual aspect of stardom. What he was looking for was a group that looked every bit as good as they sounded. More than that, they had to be dynamic, the kind of act everyone wanted to be in – desperately. Basically, what he wanted was a gang.

Now gangs get together of their own accord in playgrounds and neighbourhoods up and down the country. You don't just pick and choose 'em. But that's what happened here. It was a bit like putting a football dream team together with a big cheque-book to hand – but instead of a striker here, a defender there it was a blonde here, a brunette there. There was room for both boys and girls in this particular team, as long as they had the voice, attitude and fancy footwork needed to be Premier League material.

The line-dancing craze which was sweeping the country, taking aerobics and exercise to a new level, suggested it would be a good idea to tap (no pun intended) into something physical; from there it was just a short step to Steps. The group and its concept existed long before anyone answered the advert. With 3,000 people having answered a similar ad for Five, it was clear there were a lot of wannabe stars out there. The question was, who would answer the call?

Each of the future Steps, growing up in their own

individual neighbourhoods, knew they wanted to be someone different who stood out from the pack, without always knowing quite how and why. Certainly, none of them had pop star relations or contacts in the business. They'd have to make it their own way, with their own efforts and purely on the strength of their talent. Take Claire Richards, for instance.

Claire grew up in West London with her parents, younger sister Gemma and one very loveable dog – a collie-whippet cross called Charlie. 'He was lovely,' she recalls. She still has the same room, and it's still in the same sad state: 'pink walls, grey carpet and a load of junk!' Claire's tap and ballet lessons started at the age of four, but didn't last too long 'because they didn't have food breaks!' So Claire, along with H, is one of Steps' 'non-trained' dancers, though we hear she still has her certificate for passing Grade One ballet.

Claire kept her nose out of trouble at school – 'I was never *really* naughty' – though the occasion when she told her diabetic teacher she had a stomachache to get hold of one of the chocolate bars the teach had stashed in her desk drawer still causes just a *bit* of embarrassment. 'I forgot to have my breakfast and was really hungry,' she claims in defence, while admitting 'I still feel horrible about that now.'

Claire was a good enough singer even then to be asked to perform solos in assembly, and would sing her little heart out when the school staged end-of-year musicals. She took star roles in *The Sound Of Music* (Maria) and *Oliver* (Nancy), but as a result of all this attention some less talented people picked on her and claimed she was stuck-up. 'Because I was shy,' she explains, 'I didn't talk to many people so they all thought I was horrible.' Still, she credits her parents with teaching her to be polite and nice to people, so we reckon poor ol' Claire was just misunderstood! If she could have done with an extra friend or two, she at least had a sister – Gemma. Sad to say, the pair used to fight like cat and dog! They're best friends now, you'll be pleased to know.

If you think Claire's got a fantastic figure then you'll not be surprised to learn that her major interest when younger was athletics. At the age of nine, she was signed up by her local athletics club, which meant turning up to a lot of competitions and getting up on cold, rainy Sundays to go out on cross-country runs. Unfortunately, she had to give that lifestyle up when she developed asthma at the age of twelve – but looking back, it was certainly no bad training for the stage act that's made her and her fellow Steps famous.

Appropriately enough, given the amount of world travelling Steps have been doing recently, Claire was a prize-winning student in Geography. A model of a mountain, made with the help of her dad and uncle, won her an atlas, 'but the runners-up got money, it was so unfair!' (*Put this girl down as a future* Blue Peter *presenter! – impressed Ed.*) She also started doing drama shows with a local theatre group when she was about eleven, getting some first-hand experience of life on-stage. But her first break was . . . her wrist, when she fell over while ice skating! (*Bad joke – Ed.*)

Claire's second (less painful!) break came when at the age of seventeen she joined a girl group called TSD. The image was very much that of 'the girls next door' and Claire had shoulder-length hair at this time, a long way from the slick highlighted bob we're used to now. The group were invited on to the *Smash Hits*

Tour of 1994, and a promising career looked in prospect when they were asked to open the show for the likes of Ant and Dec, Peter Andre and Boyzone. Crowds were generous with their applause, and two minor hit singles resulted: 'Heart And Soul' which reached Number sixty-nine and 'Baby I Love You' which climbed five places higher.

It was all a long way from Claire's first job in an open-fronted greengrocer's shop where she weighed up the fruit and vegetables come sun, rain or blizzard. 'I used to spend the summers boiling hot,' she recalls, 'and in the winter I used to freeze to death!' Poor lamb!

Sadly for Claire, the end of TSD was equally uncomfortable. The news that their record company didn't want to renew their contract came in a phone-call, and she admits that at that point she felt her life was over. One of the girls she'd sung with quit on the spot, and was replaced by Mariama, who later went on to Solid Harmonie and is now Heavenlii's replacement in the Honeyz. And worse was to come, as Claire soon learned. 'I carried on with Cossie (the other girl from the original trio), but the producer we met up with wanted to work solely with her, so I felt dumped again.'

After such a double whammy, Claire's confidence was understandably at rock bottom, and she headed for the safety of a nine-to-five life. A secretarial job was hardly what dreams were made of, but Claire realized that this was real life – and she now appreciates that this early disappointment, however hard to take, has helped her keep her feet on the ground during Steps' subsequent sky-high success.

Claire stuck her new career as a temporary secretary for seven long, tedious months before she saw the ad placed in *The Stage* by Tim Byrne. Her ever-supportive mum encouraged her to go for it, even though Claire had told her she'd never sing again 'because I couldn't handle any more knock-backs.' While delighted at the way her career's taken off, she won't forget what one magazine called her 'in the dumper experience' in a hurry. 'It taught me nothing lasts forever – I'll never be big-headed about Steps because I know it could all end tomorrow. I just hope it doesn't . . .'

Lee Latchford Evans is a name we're more than familiar with these days – but the middle part is one his soccer-mad parents, Stella and Billy, gave him in honour of Everton and England star Bob Latchford, a man who was to the 1970s what Alan Shearer is to the 1990s. It's hardly surprising, then, that the athletic-looking young Lee couldn't make up his mind between a career in acting or sport. 'I always wanted to be different,' Lee admits, 'so I was a footballer and then went into theatre and started wearing tights! Everybody laughed at me, but luckily it's all paid off in the end.'

He very nearly chose football, which would have been pop's loss – scouts from Premiership club Wimbledon wanted him to come south and go on trial with them, so promising was his form in junior soccer. Instead, he decided to pursue a showbiz career. And that's where the Latchford part of his name became important, since the actors' union Equity will only allow one performer per name. Lee Evans, of course, was already taken by a certain diminutive, high-pitched comic, so Lee Latchford Evans it was. Lee grew up in Ellesmere Port, just over the river Mersey from Liverpool – hence the footballing name – and remains a keen supporter of Everton today. Could this be why Steps so often dress in blue, we wonder?

Lee's little sister Carly arrived when he was just three years old. Demonstrating an early appetite for attention, he'd do charming big-brother type things like poking her in the face with his finger when she was asleep and spraying her with an air-freshening aerosol can! It had all been so different when his granddad took him to see the newly-born Carly in hospital and there, in the cot beside her, was a toy motorbike: 'It was her present to me so I wouldn't get jealous.' Thankfully, Lee's manners with the female sex have somewhat improved these days!

The attention-seeker in Lee certainly found a way out at the school disco, where his imitation of 1980s teddy-boy hitmaker Shakin' Stevens actually won him a prize. The rocker's stage act was a bit of an imitation too, like a Welsh version of Elvis, so Lee knew exactly what he had to do – copy the King and he'd be close! 'I was there with my bright white trainers on, trembling all over the place.' The interest in music had begun when Lee was but a tiny tot. 'I'd dance every time music was put on,' he claims, adding 'I started early.' By his teens, he was playing Danny in *Grease* and setting his sights on an acting career.

The teenage Lee was something of a party animal, but fortunately for him his parents didn't really mind. In fact they more or less encouraged him. They'd head off out for a Saturday night, handing him bin bags at the door as a hint that he and his pals should tidy up after themselves . . . at least they'd know where he was! Unfortunately, other people did too. The fame of these parties travelled far and wide, and when gatecrashers arrived the boys in blue wouldn't be far behind, because bottles and cans soon started flying through the air. Lee was used to keeping one step ahead of the law, one of his favourite pastimes being 'hedge-hopping' – running through the gardens of his home estate hurdling the low hedges like a young Colin Jackson!

The worst moment of Lee's childhood came when he accidentally kicked a ball through £800-worth of windows . . . oops! 'We legged it down the street,' he recalls, 'but I was caught.' He certainly had a red face then, which would scarcely have gone with his best outfit – 'jeans with loads of brown patches on them and a blue T-shirt with a huge collar.' So that's Lee – a Scouse 'scally' with a nose for mischief and a certain lack of dress sense, but nothing too serious to worry about.

Though he claims he's been working since the tender age of nine 'as a paperboy, a barman and a shop assistant', Lee's worst pre-Steps job was as a milkman. 'In the winter,' he admitted, 'I really didn't want to get out of bed at three in the morning!' The only thing that could tempt him to get up was 'a big bowl of cornflakes!', and his brekky cereal fetish continues to this day – he'll tuck in any time, anywhere! Luckily, as time went on he spent more of his working life on-stage than in a float; at the time he was chosen to become a Step, he was about to join the cast of the West End rock opera *Tommy*. He'd previously worked with the Royal Shakespeare Company and had even appeared before royalty in a Gala Performance. The time was right for the next step . . .

Lisa Scott-Lee grew up just around the corner from Lee's native Merseyside, in North Wales – Abergele, to be precise. The oldest of four children to Jan and Tony, she was also the only girl, which means she now has pop's hunkiest fan club, in the manly shapes of brothers Stephen (aged 20), Andrew (17) and Anthony (15)!

Lisa loves her brothers to death, needless to say, but when it comes to fans, her father is right up there with the best of them. He always encouraged Lisa to go for her dreams of stardom, telling her 'You'll be all right . . . your face will be your fortune.' Surprisingly, this bit of advice used to annoy her intensely – 'I'd like to think I've got some talent as well, Dad,' was her stock answer – but today she has to admit he was a great help. Being a photographer, he has also taken a snap of every important moment in his daughter's childhood; maybe he should do a book on the growth of a star! Mum, too, encouraged her daughter to excel. 'She used to say to me, "When you're rich and famous you can do this and that," and I'd get dead excited.'

We're not saying she can swear in several languages, but Lisa is certainly fluent in Welsh, having gone to a school in an area where it was widely spoken. She's also an expert on Action Man toys, preferring to play with her brothers' 'dollies' rather than her own as a child. 'Action Man is much cooler,' she says, throwing down a challenge to Aqua and their famous 'Barbie Girl'. 'You shouldn't teach girls to be pink and fluffy and boys to be macho and hard.' Okay, with a look like that on her face we're not going to argue!

You wouldn't have called Lisa pink and fluffy, then, but she got her tomboyish self well and truly into hot water by borrowing something brown and hairy! It was a hamster she saw during a school trip to a local zoo when she was just seven. Lisa thought he looked as if he wanted to get away from it all, and she obliged, slipping him into a jacket pocket. The rodent's squeaks were a bit of a give-away, so she found herself making strange noises too so it wouldn't be noticed! But when her mum found Hammy in his new home, Lisa's little-used doll's house (its owner was obviously too busy playing with Action Men at the time), she hit the roof; and no, we're not talking the doll's house here! As for how she found out, it could have had something to do with the fact that the poor hamster was using the doll's bath as a loo!

The rodent was duly returned, but Lisa stayed embarrassed about the whole situation for at least ten years afterwards. 'I couldn't talk about it because I was so ashamed,' she sniffs, 'but I'm okay now.' Someone she undoubtedly confided in was best friend Rachel, with whom she's kept in touch despite the pressures of showbiz and whom she still phones more or less every day.

Lisa's parents certainly had to learn to be forgiving. Other tricks Lisa's owned up to since include knocking crystals off a chandelier with a tennis ball, to wear as jewellery, and sticking one of her mother's collection of china Buddha figures together after a breakage – with chewing gum, of all things! 'It must have been a professional job,' she comments, 'because Mum didn't notice anything was wrong for *weeks!*'

School encouraged her actressy ambitions, and her talents were recognized when she played Marty in *Grease* and Blousy in *Bugsy Malone*. It was clear Abergele wasn't going to be able to hold her as she swapped her first childhood ambition – of being an astronaut – for one nearer the Earth but still pretty high-flying. London was her aim, and the first stop after leaving home was the capital's famous Italia Conti stage school, where Lisa lived in a hostel with a number of other hopefuls. Ex-Eternal temptress Louise was one of her fellow pupils, though she was a couple of years older; not a bad role model to have! Lisa also got A Levels, including one in craft, design and technology, which means she's handy to have around if you need any DIY done!

At sixteen, Lisa had set her sights on having wheels – and she knew she'd have to graft to get the money. With a single-mindedness that would run all the way through her career like the word 'Blackpool' in a stick of rock, she enrolled in her local hamburger joint as a means to raise the cash. 'I'm sure I was employee of the month,' she recalls, 'but now I can only remember chicken nuggets and chips.' Once she had passed her driving test, she started ferrying her friends around in her pride and joy, bought courtesy of McDonald's. When another driver started pointing at her one night, though, she responded with a rather rude sign . . . only to hear her friend say, 'He was only telling you you'd forgotten to put your lights on!' Doh!

Lisa passed her driving test with flying colours. She also passed her audition for Steps, but had to tell a white lie so as to get time off to appear. She was the singer in a five-piece band at the time, and told her pals she was going into hospital to have her tonsils removed. 'Obviously I was singing at the time, so it was a stupid thing to say. A week later I got a record deal!'

Along with Lisa, Ian Watkins – otherwise known as H, for Hyperactive – is the second Step to be born and bred in Wales. But while Ms Scott-Lee was larging it in the north of the country, Master Watkins grew up in the Rhondda Valley, an area known in the past for its coalfields. H's was a family of blokes, apart from his mum, Gaynor; Dad Robert and brothers Jamie and

Alan could make up a rugby scrum! Talking of which, H is a very patriotic lad and loves to fly the flag for the national team. When Wales beat England in the final match of the 1999 Five Nations championship, H whipped the Welsh Dragon duvet cover off his bed and waved it for the photographers.

H was very much a home-loving lad, with a big circle of friends. And you won't be surprised to know he stays in touch with them all even today. 'Having friends you can trust around you is important,' H says, 'especially now everybody's taking an interest.' That said, he's always been a bit of a blabbermouth, and had to learn quickly the importance of keeping secrets. 'One of my friends was going out with one of my other mates and nobody was supposed to know,' he remembers, 'and I sort of let it slip. Luckily my friends soon forgave me, but my mouth runs away with me sometimes.'

When he goes back home now, no-one expects H to shell out for the drinks – even though he admits in the old days 'they used to joke that when we went for a night out I'd come home with more money than I went out with!' He discovered girls at the age of twelve, which he reckons was three years after the rest of the lads! He took a girl in his class to the cinema and, on the way home, they stopped behind a garage for a quick snog: 'It was strange,' he admits, 'but I was gagging for it!' He'd actually had loads of practice using a clay head he made in art; hope he washed his face thoroughly before approaching a real-life girl!

His hyperactive streak had people worried at one point. H tried cutting out caffeine (found in tea and coffee) and E numbers (the additives in food and drink that create bright colours), but nothing much seemed to work so he decided to enjoy being himself from then on and leave the worrying to others. 'I've always been giddy,' he says. 'I've been H since I was nine, and if I do have a tendency to jump about it's just because I'm happy being me.'

H's musical ambitions began at a tender age, when he was selected to be a choirboy. If he'd not made it in showbiz, though, he could always have become a gardener! He was given an allotment for his twelfth birthday, and went on to delight his parents by producing huge cabbages and prize-winning tomatoes! Sad to say, he also ran into trouble when he and his mates pulled up another gardener's onions; H was the only one who didn't leg it quick enough!

When the school dance took over from the allotment as the centre of young Ian Watkins' world, he made sure he was the best turned-out lad around by sneaking his mother's home-shopping catalogue into his bedroom and choosing an appropriate outfit. 'I'd order it, wear it a couple of times to the disco and then send it back. She never knew I'd done it . . .' Well, she just might now! More serious was his habit of bunking off school. H hated his schooldays – quite possibly because of his nickname, 'Swotty Watty'! He'd go in for registration, then sneak back home (just a couple of blocks away) to watch Richard and Judy on TV. 'If I got caught,' he shamefacedly admits, 'I just wrote a note saying I'd been to the doctor or dentist and signed my parents' signatures on the bottom.' Oo-er, don't try this at home, or school, kids!

Coincidentally, the first group H ever idolized was a five-piece boy-girl band called Five Star. It helped that he had a crush on Doris, one of the three sisters in the group, though he admits he wouldn't have passed up a snog with Kylie or even Siobhan from Bananarama. His party piece from the age of six was 'The Land Of Make Believe' by Bucks Fizz, and by the time he was ten he'd graduated to that traditional crowd-pleaser 'You Are My Sunshine', which won him a prize in a holiday camp talent show!

If H started his performing life at an early age, perhaps it was because of his deficiencies in the sports department. Unlike future Steps-mate Lee, he was hopeless at football and was *always* – but always – the last one to be picked in the playground when teams were organized for the unofficial twenty-a-side 'football' tournaments (played with a tennis ball). These days, he's much in demand for celebrity tournaments – so something's gone very right! Look out Michael Owen, we say.

Had he not been lured by showbiz, H would have carried on at art college. He'd got an A grade in his art GCSE and had done his foundation course before he made the decision to pack it all in; we have a sneaking feeling he'll carry on with his art later in life. In fact, we hear H has designed a new Steps logo which has yet to be used . . .

H chose the ideal job to keep his showbiz talents finely honed – he became a Butlins Redcoat! While most aspiring singers and actors have to eke out a living between jobs by waiting tables or temping, H was being paid to entertain. There can't be too many of us who haven't sampled life at a holiday camp, and if you have you'll know that the red-coated hosts work tirelessly day and night to make sure your stay is a memorable one. Well, H was certainly no exception to that rule, and could look at the likes of Shane Ritchie and Bradley Walsh as two ex-Redcoats who have gone on to find national fame.

Holidays, of course, are fun – but schooldays for Faye Tozer, the fifth member of the Steps team-to-be, were pretty eventful too. The first time she got into big trouble was when a teacher caught her climbing up the walls in the girls' loos. 'I had to wash the walls as punishment,' she confesses gloomily, 'it was horrible.' Things went downhill from there. Another school memory was of a report that sums up her chatty nature. 'Faye talks too much and must not be allowed to sit next to her friend, Lisa Valentine, any more. We will not warn her again!'

The big love of Faye's life, and the one thing that made all the aggravation worthwhile, was dancing. She'd started classes at the tender age of six, where she met her best friend Taryn, and would meet another long-time pal, Lulabelle, when they later studied together at dance school. Faye was more than just enthusiastic – she was a real child prodigy, and started teaching classes at the tender age of fourteen. In her 'special thanks' on the first album, she credits Anne Gale's School of Dance for the 'priceless training' she received.

When Faye came home from classes, her mum used to sit her down on a chair and make her sing any new song she'd learned. And school productions utilized the leggy lovely's undoubted talents. 'I was always a dancer,' she recalls. 'I didn't get my first acting part until I was eleven.' By then, she had all the signs of an all-round entertainer.

She idolized Rick Astley, the handsome crooner who topped the charts back in 1987 with 'Never Gonna Give You Up'. Her bedroom walls were permanently papered with posters of the adorable Mr A, and as coincidence would have it she would later work with his producer, Pete Waterman. In fact, Rick popped into the studio when Steps were recording *Step One* and asked if anyone fancied a take-away meal! Sadly, all Faye could say (apart from 'Prawn Madras and a box of poppadams') was 'He's gone for that rough look, now . . . he didn't look as good as he used to!'

But the days of rubbing shoulders with the stars were still a long way off. Growing up with a sister called Claire also prepared Faye for life as a Step, though Claire's two years older and, as she herself admits, Faye's complete opposite. When Faye was fifteen they fell out big-time and blows were exchanged: 'I decked her and she went *mad!*' Faye remembers. Happily, opposites ended up attracting (once the bruises faded!), and Claire's now a frequent backstage visitor at Steps concerts. She also has a thing for boy bands, so sisterly introductions are most welcome!

The first time Faye put on her disco-dancing shoes was at the age of twelve, when she glammed up to go to a disco organized for under-eighteens. She recalls 'running round, snogging as many boys as possible' before her dad turned up to drag her kicking and screaming back home! You might gather from this that Faye hung around with an older crowd, and you'd be right. By the time she turned eighteen, though, most of them had already left the neighbourhood and her coming of age party was one of the worst-attended events in history!

While waiting for stardom to strike, Faye had been cooking pizza at Whipsnade Zoo (for people, not animals, we presume!), but she decided the big city had more opportunities to show what she could cook up on the dancing, singing and acting fronts. Even though she knew she had to move to follow her dream, Faye found it a real wrench to leave her family. 'I moved away when I was about eighteen,' she recalls, 'lived abroad for two years and ever since I've been back we've been getting closer and closer.'

Having returned to London, Faye was fronting a band at the Park Lane Hilton in the centre of town when the chance to audition for Steps came up. 'I was singing in an upstairs cocktail bar wearing sequins from head to toe.' The uniform may have changed, but the talent most certainly hasn't! And when Steps booked up for July 1999's Party In the Park at Hyde Park, not a stone's throw from the Hilton, it gave Faye a chance to walk down memory lane and enjoy the thought of how far she'd come in just a couple of years. It had seemed a risk at the time to exchange guaranteed money for a chance of stardom, but it had paid off handsomely (*I wonder if she'd like to do my lottery numbers? – Ed*).

You've now caught up with what the five Steps members were doing before they answered that fateful newspaper ad. Five individuals were about to be moulded into an entertainment machine – and manager Tim Byrne was to perform this task along with co-manager Vicky Blood, a New Zealander with considerable experience in the pop business. As Steps prepared to release their first single at the end of 1997, the charts were still full of mellow ballads, middle-aged music and the Teletubbies. The likes of Hanson, Eternal and Aqua seemed to be fighting a losing battle to liven things up. Call the cavalry . . . call for Steps!

FAMOUS FIVE

There's no such thing as an overnight success – and though it seemed Steps suddenly appeared in our charts as if by magic, a whole lot of hard work had gone on behind the scenes to make them the showbiz hotshots they'd become. Much of it happened in the year after manager Tim Byrne got the famous five together – a year in which the record producer, record company, promotions machine and, most importantly, the group, were honed and polished to pop perfection.

Steps' producer was to be Peter Waterman, the pop maestro whose previous clients had included Kylie and Jason, Bananarama, Rick Astley and Donna Summer. 'We've had three years of gloom and despondency,' he said, pointing to the charts. 'It's just been dire. The world's depressing enough . . . it's time to do what we do best.'

The launch pad was '5,6,7,8', an up-tempo dance tune that owed its existence to the country and western line-dancing craze which had been sweeping Britain for the past few months. Leisure centres and village halls had been packed to the rafters with people 'getting down' to the new pastime that combined dancing with aerobics. It had been invented in the States, where country music is king – but anything with a beat and a boot-scootin' tempo was fair game. That's where Steps came in.

The video was shot in Spain a matter of days after the group came together, and Australians took to the beach-side location so much that they made the single a chart-topper. For the group, it was 'like a little holiday at the start of everything'. Little did they know what lay around the corner – because once back at Heathrow, their feet had barely touched the tarmac before the whirl of personal appearances began!

The first was at London's trendy Atlantic Bar, where Steps were booked to do a showcase for the media. *Smash Hits* magazine managed to turn up late, so the five happily went back up on-stage to give them a special command performance. They'd be richly rewarded, too: the *Smash Hits* Tour of 1997 would give the group some much-appreciated exposure as the warm-up act for bigger names, while they'd be headliners on the same jaunt twelve short but hit-filled months later.

But back to '5,6,7,8': Faye admits it was the fact that the song was different that attracted her to it. The record showed amazing stamina, entering the Top 20 in mid-November and peaking at Number 14 in the first week of 1998. The wave of pre-Christmas releases from star names kept pushing Steps down, but they just wouldn't be denied. Television couldn't get enough of them, and the record made a record of its own by being the biggest-selling single of the 1990s to peak outside the Top 10.

For Faye, Lee, H, Claire and Lisa, the world had suddenly turned upside down. From being five little-known showbiz hopefuls, they suddenly found themselves doing their line dance on any show worth its salt, from *Top Of The Pops* to *Blue Peter* and all points in-between. Happily, the next single, 'Last Thing On My Mind', required another exotic video, so the group managed to squeeze in a trip to the Caribbean island of Cuba where their poolside antics made for another great vid. It was clear that Steps were on for their first Top 10 entry, and 'Last Thing . . .' didn't disappoint, shooting straight into the listings at Number 6 in early May.

It would bow out six weeks and 200,000 copies later, and its success gave them two bites at *Top Of The Pops* this time. But Steps were now a group in demand. They juggled their schedule to promote their successful single all over Europe as well as recording tracks for their first album, while invitations to film premieres and other swanky events came flooding in. The MTV Awards saw them mingling with Madonna, George Michael and fashion designer Jean-Paul Gaultier, and while it was a thrill to see such famous people in the flesh, Claire admitted it made the group realize they still had a way to go.

The recording sessions for *Step One* (their debut album) certainly took their toll on Steps' vocal cords, and huge quantities of Ribena were consumed in an attempt to make sure the tenth 'take' was as tuneful as the first; Pete Waterman (the hit-making producer) is nothing if not a perfectionist! Amazingly, Steps' fame had spread to such an extent that any time the tour bus pulled up outside Waterman's south London studios for a session there was at least a handful of long-suffering supporters there to wish them luck. It did wonders for morale, especially when the fabulous five were dead on their feet and ready to drop.

The important thing, Lee emphasized, was for

people to still accept them as normal people. 'It's quite nice, 'cos we're keeping our feet on the ground, not walking round in a big pop star strop with shades and bodyguards.' So autographs were signed, hugs exchanged and the foundations built for a great relationship between Steps and their fanatical followers that continues to this day. The fans all know that H covets stuffed toys, that Lisa appreciates sweets to suck on those long, boring airline flights and that Faye . . . well, let's not give away all the secrets, shall we?

Back to *Step One*, and with so many quality tracks to choose from, there was no shortage of candidates for Steps' next single. In the end the choice went to 'One For Sorrow' – a song which gave Claire the vocal spotlight. It also offered the five Steps the chance to top up their tan by picnicking in a field of sunflowers in Italy. Sadly for them, and unknown to viewers, it was on the windward side of a sewage works, so the biggest challenge was to keep disgusted looks off their faces as they mimed away. Another unsuspected hazard lay in the huge number of snakes, slugs and creepy-crawlies lurking in the grass.

The song, though, was a fabulous romp whose sheer danceability got over the tear-jerking lyric, delivered by Ms Richards with great style. It was the ideal summer sound, so its release in August was spot-on. Rumours in the record biz suggested Steps were on course for a seasonal chart-topper, but they'd reckoned without the Manic Street Preachers, whose new single ('If You Tolerate This Your Children Will Be Next') happened to coincide with the fab fivesome's release. What the heck, Number 2 is higher than most bands ever reach, and for a third single it was something really special. With nearly 150,000 copies of their biggest hit passing over the counter in the first week of sales (it would go on to top the million mark), Steps were now truly a household name.

But could the album do better? Again, it was the Manics who stood in their way, and even though James Dean Bradfield's mum bought the Steps album (much to her son's displeasure) the Welsh group came in on top. At least Steps had the pleasure of pushing the Corrs back down to Number 3!

Things were going off the scale by now on the fame front, and none of Steps could venture outside their front doors without being besieged by autograph-hunting admirers. The ever-hyperactive H even had to invest in some relaxation tapes so as not to go completely over the top. And there was to be no hiding place anywhere in the world – Australia, where '5,6,7,8' had been a major hit, was crying out for a piece of the action. High time we paid them back for *Neighbours* and *Home And Away!* Steps spent a full three days there in September in a flying visit to celebrate 'Last Thing On My Mind' topping the Aussie charts, then returned home via Hong Kong and Thailand to enjoy a well-earned two-day holiday!

Safely back in the good ol' UK, Claire pinpoints the release of 'Heartbeat'/'Tragedy' in November as the moment it all went ballistic. 'People were staring at me, following me in and out of shops, even coming up to me when I was queuing for my Kentucky Fried Chicken!', she recalls. Faye was accosted while buying her underwear in Marks and Spencer, while H insists he wore a Father Christmas beard 'and *still* got recognized!'

Maybe the videos had something to do with it. Each song of the double-sided single got its own video, but each one was very different. 'Heartbeat' had a seasonably snowy setting, and took two days to shoot – the most expensive Steps video so far – while 'Tragedy' gave the girls' real-life dads the chance to walk them up the aisle. According to Claire, none of them were 'planning real-life weddings just yet,' which was doubtless good news for all their male fans.

The biggest thrill of the pre-Christmas period was playing the *Smash Hits* Poll Winners' Party for the second consecutive year – though it was their first as a big-name act. In 1997, they'd been told there was no time for them to rehearse. This time, though, everyone found a reason to be in the hall as Steps sorted out their dance moves; the band even got a round of applause at the end. 'I remember thinking, "Ooh, that's different",' says an obviously appreciative Lee.

The performance of 'Heartbeat'/'Tragedy' in the singles chart was quite remarkable. By linking one of *Step One*'s standout tracks with an otherwise unavailable cover version of a Bee Gees chart-topping classic from 1979, Steps' record company Jive had come up with the perfect proposition; even if you bought the album, you just had to have this! It was also the ideal Christmas present for anyone with an interest in great pop music, and while a year earlier '5,6,7,8' had been blocked from its rightful Top 10 place by the sheer weight of big-name releases in the queue, this double whammy of a single was clearly made of sterner stuff.

The single had entered the chart on 21 November behind Cher's 'Believe', then on week four of a seven-week stay. It seemed possible the fab five might make the all-important step (sorry!) to the summit, but the next week saw them descend four places like an express lift. Not only had Cher refused to yield, but new releases by Five, Celine Dion (with R Kelly) and the Vengaboys had shot into places two, three and four. With the Corrs coming up fast behind them, Steps looked down and on the way out!

They gamely hung in there, though, and although they slipped as far as Number 8, they'd clawed their way back to Number 6 by Boxing Day. In pole position at this stage were the Spice Girls, with Chef from *South Park* and Denise and Johnny, good pals of Steps from *The Big Breakfast*, second and third. What next? What was next came on 9 January, when Steps – thanks to heavy TV play of those two videos we talked about – found themselves on top of the singles pile for the first time ever.

As they set out on their 'Step One' tour, their first nationwide jaunt, Steps had to get used to being protected from over-zealous fans who just couldn't wait to get their hands on their heroes. 'Even though we sell loads and loads of records,' said Claire, 'I'd just like us to be treated in the same way as other groups who haven't sold as many.' Steps were very keen not to be seen as aloof by the people they worked with. Faye remembered watching All Saints 'and everybody around them, even their dancers, were a bit precious with them. We just get on stage and it's like, "All right, mate?" Everyone just carries on mucking around.'

But the burden of fame was getting heavier month by month. By the time 'Better Best Forgotten' was released in February 1999, Steps found themselves celebrating their third front cover of *Smash Hits*, the style bible for any self-respecting teenager. No chance of anonymity now! On the other hand, this had been H's dream since he was knee-high to a grasshopper. And Faye admits that when she went into supermarkets and petrol stations, she wasn't averse to putting *Smash Hits* at the front of the magazine pile!

It seemed that the only places Steps could wander without too much fear of being mobbed by fans were occasions like the Brits, where they rubbed shoulders with other stars. There was quite a kerfuffle at the Brit Awards in 1999, where Steps were booked to appear as part of an Abba tribute. Radio 1 listeners had voted for their favourite new group, who would be awarded a Brit – the only statuette whose destination is decided by a democratic vote of fans rather than the big-wigs of the biz.

It was leaked a few days before the ceremony that Steps would be getting the gong, so acceptance speeches were practised in front of five mirrors as the big day dawned. Come the night of the awards, though, the destination of the coveted prize had changed, and was heading north of the border to little-known Belle and Sebastian. Everyone was shocked, to put it mildly, and the accusation that multiple voting via the Internet had tipped the scales in B&S's favour only added fuel to the fire. 'Everyone who won has got guitars,' sniffed Lee, 'but that's the business, I suppose. I like the fact that when they announced the winner nobody cheered 'cos no-one knows who they are!'

In the end, the British Phonographic Industry, the organisation behind the Brits, upheld the result, though it seemed extra safeguards might well be put in place for the 2000 poll. And when *The Sun* ran their own telephone poll (which Steps, needless to say, won by a mile), honour was satisfied.

The next step for Steps was to record a second album – and having found such success first time out there was no way they were going to fiddle with a winning formula! As before, the songs were put together during gaps in Steps' busy schedule, and by June the first six tracks had been completed to Pete Waterman's satisfaction.

A new single would be released to brighten up the summer months, entitled 'Love's Got A Hold On My Heart' – 'very disco, and very Steps' – said *Smash Hits* magazine, their ear to the studio door. Other highlights-to-be included 'Deeper Shade Of Blue', 'I Surrender', 'Never Say Never Again' – the most Abba-esque of the tracks so far – and 'Make It Easy On Yourself'. The last-named was already being spoken of in hushed terms as a future single, while Steps were rumoured to have the Christmas 1999 Number 1 sewn up with 'When I Said Goodbye', a slushy duet between H and Claire. We just can't wait to see the Millennium out with Steps.

June 1999 also saw the band get their fourth *Smash Hits cover.* But hang on – there's only one face on it! It was H, the 'Clown Prince Of Pop', who revealed all inside about his 'failed auditions, tears, heartache and meditation' under the title 'Tears of a Clown'. He revealed he'd learned how to juggle and walk tightropes when he performed in a production of the stage show *Barnum*, that he and Lisa had bonded straight away 'because we were the Welshies', and that he doesn't think he's a pop star, 'I'm just doing a job.'

That's as may be, but what a job! Lee was particularly happy that the hotel rooms Steps get these days are absolutely palatial. 'It does make a change from the old days when we'd have to do a gig in a club in Blackpool, then drive back to London that night.' He wouldn't have to do too much travelling to

Steps' biggest concert of 1999, scheduled for Hyde Park in London on American Independence Day, 4 July – the Party In The Park, in which they'd share a stage with Boyzone, the Corrs and 1980s chart-toppers Culture Club.

The fact that Lee could hoof it to Hyde Park was just as well – because, unfortunately for him, his arrival at the launch party for the concert, held exactly a month beforehand, was forty-five minutes late! He got off the tube at the wrong station, leaving Lisa, H and pal Gary Barlow fretting outside. 'Lee got lost,' said a band spokesman, 'and was wandering around London trying to find his way to Hyde Park!' Publicity pictures saw Lisa looking extremely brassed off, Gary confused and H grinning goofily as per usual!

They'd be rubbing shoulders in the greenery with the likes of the Pet Shop Boys, Another Level and Latin American sensation Ricky Martin. Radio and TV stations were battling for rights to broadcast the event, which seemed likely to give Steps their biggest worldwide audience ever. That might cheer Lisa up a bit!

With *Step One* already well into seven-figure sales in Britain alone, a new album all but finished and a fan-following verging on the super-dedicated, Steps face the new Millennium in the greatest of shape. There won't be too many days off to look forward to, but that's the least of their worries. Five-strong, footloose and full of energy, the Steps machine is going flat out – and it won't stop until the whole world is conquered!

STEPS STYLE

Every group has to have an image, but Steps are one outfit that gives its members a little bit of licence to wear what they fancy. On-stage, it's inevitably stuff that looks good and matches – blue for the girls, dark colours for the lads – and Steps even have a stylist, Sophie, to do the legwork. But we've seen enough of Steps 'out of uniform' to know that they have their own styles to bring to the party.

FAYE

Faye has become known as the Step who has a thing about her hairstyle. Her dreadlock hair extensions were the talk of pop, and she admits the more people make a fuss about it the more tempted she is to do something even dafter! She adopted the dreadlocks after meeting soul singer Billy Ocean, best remembered for the original version of Boyzone's 'When The Going Gets Tough'.

Faye's a girl who knows the kind of image she wants to portray – and goes all out to get it. Take her 'dizzy blonde' look. 'Faye has totally reinvented herself,' comments Lisa. 'You should see her passport photo – she used to have really long, curly, dark blonde hair and a bit more puppy fat. She's much more gorgeous now.' Ask the lady herself and she'll admit 'I'm not naturally this blonde, but being blonde makes me feel a bit sunnier.'

Her biggest change in style since becoming famous is upping the quality of the make-up she uses. Faye now lays out on Christian Dior and Hard Candy, instead of the 'cheap, skanky stuff' she used to use when times were tough.

Faye admits she's a real serial shopper and even back in the old days used to hit the town with her friends on a Saturday 'not to hang around in McDonald's or anything, just full-on shopping!' These days, accessories are found at swankier emporia – most notably a boutique called Hype in Kensington, where Faye finds 'nice little bits and bobs and designer-y things.'

When she's slipping on her shoes for a night out, Faye isn't properly dressed unless she's got at least a three-inch heel, and preferably a bit of a platform to go with it! What goes up, though, must come down, and Faye bitterly remembers hopping round on one stiletto heel when she boogied too hard and her shoe fell apart!

They call Faye the golden girl of Steps – and to prove it she's been known to buy self-tanning lotion by Clarins to slap on when she can't get the real thing (sun, that is!). Faye's such a sun worshipper that she's even been known to sunbathe with no top on – though she recommends packing and using Mr Men sun cream to avoid burns where it hurts!

Faye's energy and vitality come from within – and she makes sure it stays that way by taking loads of vitamin C each and every morning to ward off germs. 'I take oily vitamins for my bones and multi-vitamins for my all-over health,' she glows, 'but vitamins cost a fortune these days!' That's true, but doesn't she look well on it! On the other hand, if you hear a strange rattling as Steps go through their paces, you'll know who it is!

H

'I wouldn't wear posh clothes even if I could!' declares H, who nevertheless admits he's been coaxed into shops like Harvey Nicks in the past. His early trademark was a monkey T-shirt, of which he's acquired four to date. He seems just as happy in a plain top and jeans as in anything flashy or designer-like, but whatever it is, make it colourful: 'I'm not ready to wear black yet!' he smiles.

His hairstyle may look deceptively simple, too, but H is in the toppermost snipping league these days. 'I used to get my hair cut for £2.50,' he complains good-naturedly, 'and now it costs £90!' It can't be that bad, though – he passed the name of his hairdresser on to Claire! His worst ever haircut involved bleaching the top of his hair and having the back permed – eucch! H's floppy blonde hair is his most recognisable feature, though, apart from that smile, and he finds if he puts a hat on 'people will talk to me as a person . . . I just call myself Ian.'

H is the one Step who doesn't turn brown in the sun – and he doesn't care in the slightest! A tan is not his cup of tea, and he's not bothered about the 'polar bear' jibes he gets. When it comes to cosmetics he's very down to earth, preferring Boots' own brand shampoo to anything TV-advertised and costly. Food-wise, he's tried all sorts of exotic grub as Steps have munched their way round the world, but the key to success for this particular Step is 'ketchup on everything'.

Footwear for H has to be strictly practical. He admits to having amassed a gigantic collection of trainers, but when you're famous you get given quite a few things and we doubt he's shelled out for all of 'em. Not that he'll wear anything but his current favourites. When H, Claire and Lisa shared a flat, the cry was always going up: 'Where's me trainers?' because H is a mite forgetful. And it's not just his shoes, either: his wallet was once found in the fridge-freezer, of all places.

H is currently on a fitness kick which involves 'using this abs thing to try and give me muscles. I'm no Lee Steps, but that's kinda good 'cos I'm the opposite – I've got a bit of a flabby belly.' That pot should soon disappear if he keeps up his jogging and the dreaded sit-ups. Maybe he needs Mr Motivator . . .

That's the body taken care of (we hope), but the most important piece of exercise H is going in for involves his mind. 'For the last six months I've done meditation,' he says, 'and that clears the head. It's very relaxing, and you shouldn't knock it until you've tried it.' So is this the end for Hyperactive Steps and the beginning of Blissed-out Steps? We'll have to wait and see!

CLAIRE

To look at Claire now and compare her with the young star-to-be who sang with TSD, the difference is astounding. Okay, she's had the straggly hair cut short into a smart style, but it's the all-round poise and assurance that really makes the difference. The hair, incidentally, is courtesy of classy Covent Garden crimpers Macmillans, where Claire had no fewer than three colours put in. She claims it cost her over £100, and that's including a 20 per cent discount for being famous!

When it comes to make-up, Claire's never been one to save money. She goes for the full monty, including 'brushes and brush cleaner, all the useless stuff that I never use!' Little wonder Faye admits 'We all use Claire's stuff. She has all the latest gadgets and make-up.' Favourite brands include Lancome and Mac, which we warn you won't give you much change out of your pocket money!

As far as clothes go, Claire's stage gear is bought by Steps stylist Sophie, but when it comes to day-to-day wear, she's more than happy to take the credit. 'I'll shop anywhere I can,' she says, adding 'I absolutely love it!' She's never lost her eye for value, and even though she's now in the designer bracket, Claire will certainly not pass up a bargain. *Live And Kicking* magazine once let Steps loose in London's Camden Market to see what they could find for £20, and Claire managed to come back with combat trousers and matching top in her bag. Unfortunately, she'd gone £5 over budget, but Lisa helped her out by lending her a fiver!

When she goes out at night, Claire reckons it's important to make the effort to be glam. She uses glitter on her shoulders and cleavage so she shimmers and sparkles in those disco lights! Talking of lights, she's often to be seen wearing her sunglasses 'when I've had a late night'. Experts say drinking plenty of water is the best way to avoid a hangover after those late party nights, and Claire has found you should definitely apply it to the inside, not the outside. 'At a gig H started flicking water at me. I chucked some back and ran out, but I tripped up on a step and flew through the air. Instead of helping me, H tipped the whole bottle of water over my head!'

You won't see Claire in skirts – not if she can help

it, anyway! 'I've got horrible legs!' she groans. So it's slacks and strappy tops for Ms Richards, if you please. In some ways though, she'd like the luxury of being able to stay in her pyjamas all day. 'I like to recharge my batteries, watch the television, have a bath and listen to my CDs. I've never been a party person.' Beauty sleep is important to this beauty, but someone had better tell Steps' tour manager – ooh, those early morning calls!

LEE

At first sight you might think that Lee is a stereotypical northerner, someone who knows the value of money and spends it with extreme caution. In fact, that couldn't be much further from the truth. When it comes to clothes, he is very much a believer in the adage that you get what you pay for. 'If you buy a coat for £5,' he says sagely, 'it'll probably last you about five weeks, whereas if you pay £100 it'll last you 100 weeks.' Little wonder, then, that he's a designer label man, right down to the Calvin Klein underwear!

When disaster struck and his suitcase was lost in the Philippines, Lee had to wear H's clothes for three days. 'I've never looked so bad!' he groans. Considering their tastes differ so widely, right down to Lee's preference for loafers as opposed to H's ever-present trainers, it's amazing they can both exist in the same room, let alone in the same group! Our advice is to hang on to your bag in future . . .

Clothes aside, Lee would be worth quite a bit if you melted him down, thanks to a collection of solid sterling silver jewellery he keeps about his person. Look carefully, for instance, and you'll find an ear clip nestling snugly towards the top of his right ear, while elsewhere on his body can be found a silver necklace, silver rings and his latest acquisition, a silver watch.

It's very important for Lee to stay in tip-top condition, and he makes sure he stays that way by investigating the gym facilities at any hotel that Steps book into. As H remarks, the rest of them are often to be found in the jacuzzi, waving at him! Once he gets out, he's particular about how he smells, and Polo Sport is his current approved eau de cologne/after shave.

Lee's hair is his crowning glory, and if Steps are booked to do four things in a day – a TV show, photo-shoot what-have-you – Lee will make sure he does his hair that many times. Not that he'd admit it to his bandmates! 'He insists we have a sink available everywhere we go,' hoots Lisa, 'and he won't go on stage unless he's had it done!' Over to the defence: 'I'm not vain, but I like to think my hair looks good,' Lee snorts, running a little bit of gel through his dark locks to keep everything in place.

Unfortunately, Lee sometimes gets carried away while shopping, and admits he was worried when the alarms went off as he was leaving Cecil Gee's, a well-known men's outfitters. Had he accidentally put something in his bag without realizing it? Thankfully, the only problem was the assistant had forgotten to take the security tag off a (paid-for) T-shirt. It was almost as embarrassing as when Lee went into Top Man and came face to face with a shop dummy wearing exactly the same clothes as him! With that in mind, we reckon the alarm was picking out a man with good taste!

LISA

It doesn't matter what Lisa wears, she'll always be the little girl in the tutu to her dear old mum! 'She's got this picture of me on the sideboard at home,' Lisa explains. 'I'm about nine and I'm wearing a pink ballet tutu and pink tights. Everyone says it's cute but I think it's really embarrassing!'

We don't know if Gianni Versace makes tutus (*doubt it very much – Ed*), but his dresses are far more Lisa's style these days. She managed to lay her hands on one when Steps were doing a photo-shoot and, amazingly, was allowed to keep it! Otherwise she's as happy in skirts as in trousers, and with a figure like hers, who wouldn't show off in a scoop-neck top?

Lisa's pretty conservative when it comes to what she puts on her feet, admitting to owning 'twenty pairs of socks – and they're all black!' Having tried to dance in five-inch heels, she now wears sensible trainers at all times. But her best-remembered footwear was the platform boot she once waved at an airline flight attendant who mentioned that footwear could not be worn in the event of an emergency landing – these were shoes you could parachute off!

Perfume-wise, she insists on Coconut from the Body Shop, and isn't too happy when she has to settle for less. Claire calls it her 'pulling perfume', while H claims it 'reminds you of tropical beaches'. As for hairspray, her enemies might claim Lisa's trying to punch a hole in the ozone layer. 'She goes through tons and tons of the stuff,' explains Lee, who recommends standing in her vicinity if you want your hair to behave – 'stick your head near her and you don't need to buy any!'

With an extensive wardrobe of on-stage and off-stage gear that could happily clothe an average girl's school, it's all a long way from Lisa's own schooldays. Back in Abergele in the early 1990s, she admits she favoured the Goth look with black everything – lip liner, lipstick, nail varnish, the lot! Happily it was a phase that only lasted a couple of weeks! We haven't seen her in Doc Martens recently, either . . .

Lisa dares to bare, as can be seen from the sleeve shot for 'Last Thing On My Mind' for which she shows a flash of tanned tum in a skimpy two-piece. Yet she's always felt a bit nervous wearing boob tubes ever since the day one let her down at the school disco. Since she was about nine at the time, she doubts if anyone noticed!

When it comes to nightwear, Lisa's love of pyjamas is legendary – so much so that she's even been seen wearing them in motorway service stations! It's a Steps tradition to buy Lisa pyjamas for her birthday, and last year's presents saw a lot of use. Remember, remember the fifth of November. But don't ever mention that photo: it's tutu much!

MUSICAL STEPS

Steps' sales success simply can't be doubted. *Step One* is currently four times platinum in Britain (over 1.2 million copies sold) while their five singles to date have clocked up figures in the millions. Not bad for a group no one had even heard of two years ago! The sound is contemporary, fresh and highly danceable, thanks to the vocal talents of the fivesome and the mastery of the teams of writers and studio wizards they've worked with.

Steps are most often compared to Eurovision outfits – Abba, Bucks Fizz and the like – who had a similar boy-girl line-up. Yet the pizzazz in their music that's added by producers like Pete Waterman belongs first and foremost on the dance floor. Maybe people should just accept Steps as what they are – utterly unique!

Another favourite theory is that Steps are producers' puppets because they don't write their own songs, simply singing what they're told to. This is a criticism that's harder than most to disprove, since only those in the studio can verify what the individual Steps add to the songs they perform. Suffice to say for now that all the members of Steps write as well as sing, and Lee is hopeful there'll be self-penned material on the next album.

Claire for one isn't that bothered if people don't take Steps seriously – that's their loss, she reckons. 'We don't know how we're going to develop,' she says of the future. 'In a few years we may want to make it more successfully – who knows?' For Lee, it's a question of 'doing what we want – and we want our crowd to come with us.' Lisa puts it down to 'a lot of talent and a winning formula'.

The group members' favourite records are as varied as they are. Amusingly, Faye goes for a Eurovision outfit – but not the obvious one! 'Walking On Sunshine' was a 1985 Top 10 hit for 1997 winners Katrina and the Waves. Lee and Claire are both major fans of Will Smith, the *Independence Day* actor who just can't help getting jiggy with us! They plump for his ode to 'Summertime', recorded with musical confederate Jazzy Jeff when Will was still best known for his TV portrayal of the Fresh Prince of Bel Air.

When you've got a hyperactive character, you could be expected to go for a 'happy house' type track as one of your all-time favourite records. H, though, has never lacked the ability to surprise us, and goes for 'Set Adrift On Memory Bliss', the smoochy PM Dawn hit from 1991 that samples Spandau Ballet rather a lot. Staying in a mellow summertime mood, Lisa likes 'Just Another Day' by Latin superstar Jon Secada, once upon a time a backing musician for Gloria Estefan but now a big name in his own right.

H is a big fan of the stunning Mariah Carey, whose 'My All' is a favourite. 'It reminds me of when I was in love with somebody,' he sniffs, 'and it was really, really nice. And I loved the video as well – it was gorgeous.' Not that H is always so soft-centred:

he's been known to do a mean version of Barry Manilow's 'Copacabana' when in karaoke mood!

When he was younger Master Watkins was keen on Take That, and especially likes 'Pray' and 'A Million Love Songs'. He'd have been a great asset to any boy band himself, and is one of the few people we can think of who'd have slotted into Robbie Williams' vacant space without any trouble at all! He once tried to get Kavana to accompany him in a karaoke version of Rod Stewart's 'Da Ya Think I'm Sexy?', which gives some idea of his dodgy musical taste (*only joking, H! – Ed*).

Claire's a sucker for the big ballad, and one of the thrills of her Steps life was meeting Celine Dion when she was rehearsing. 'I got so excited,' she admits. It all fits in with her mellow off-stage mood. Lee doesn't care for indie rock, and complains that no-one takes Steps seriously 'cos they don't play guitars. Well, a guitar would get in the way of the dance moves, wouldn't it?

Lisa's musical preferences are dance and garage music, and she admits she'd never have bought '5,6,7,8' if she hadn't been on the record. 'I would definitely have bought "Tragedy" and "Heartbeat", though,' she says of their double-sided chart-topper, ''cos they're wicked songs!' (She's met the Bee Gees, who originally recorded 'Tragedy', and describes them as 'true professionals'.) There aren't many types of song she's not tried herself, in her various jobs in cabaret, stage musicals and the like.

Faye's previous 'life' singing in a show band at a swish London hotel means she can sing the standards – 'The Way We Were', 'Don't Cry For Me Argentina', all that kind of slushy stuff – with professional ease. Claire, on the other hand, says listening to Karen

Carpenter (the late, great American singer) was the reason she started singing. If she could choose to interview any pop star still alive today, she says she'd probably choose Prince.

The girls always get in the mood before a big night out by blasting out some of their favourite sounds on a ghetto-blaster: Brandy and Monica, either separately or together, are firm favourites. They draw the line at singing into hairbrushes, though! 'We're professionals!' they squeal. Lisa likes 'anything with a really good beat', and is also partial to No Doubt's 'Don't Speak' – a chart-topper in anyone's language!

Lee's listening preferences are wide indeed (*they'd have to be if they include Shakin' Stevens! – sarky Ed*). That's why he goes for compilation CDs, which Steps find themselves on rather a lot these days, of course! He's also very partial to rock ballads like Aerosmith's 'I Don't Want To Miss A Thing' from Bruce Willis's *Armageddon* – possibly 'cos Lisa says she waves her knickers in the air to it!

The best way for Steps to grab a large chunk of credibility might well be to sing the signature tune to a trendy TV programme. It's no coincidence they perform the *Friends* theme on stage, and to be associated with a series like that or *Dawson's Creek* would do them no harm at all. Another possibility would be to link with another act for a joint single, as they did with the Abba project. Faye and H both want to get together with the Backstreet Boys, and since they're both on the same record label, Jive, there's every chance that a collaboration could come off.

It seems to be the way these days that group members take time out to do their own solo thing – think of Ronan Keating and his contribution to the *Notting Hill* soundtrack. It'd be interesting to see what happened if Steps tried it, but the nearest thing we can imagine is H and Claire's forthcoming duet on the Christmas 1999 single. However, as we well know, Steps have already guested as a group on something . . .

The tribute single 'Thank Abba For The Music' gave Steps a way to pay tribute to the superstar Swedes on the 25th anniversary of their Eurovision win. They joined forces with B*Witched, Cleopatra, Tina Cousins and Billie to camp it up in platform heels for the 1999 Brit Awards, and were delighted when the medley of Abba classics, released as a single by public demand, shot up the charts to peak at Number 4. In the wake of all this publicity, the compilation 'Abba Gold' was reissued in an anniversary edition and found itself at the very top of the charts. It wasn't the first time Steps had covered Abba – at the karaoke party to celebrate the end of the 1998 *Smash Hits* tour, they kicked off proceedings with 'Dancing Queen'. 'Everyone says we sound like Abba,' laughed Lisa at the time, 'so we might as well do this one.'

Having done their bit to help the Abba revival, Steps were very happy to be invited to the premiere of a London musical based entirely round Abba songs. *Mamma Mia* opened at the Prince Edward Theatre in the West End, and afterwards the famous five – well, four actually, 'cos Faye was unwell, poor love! – were happy to relive their favourite bits. 'The storyline's about a daughter who wants to get married,' explained Lee, 'and the soundtrack is Abba songs.' Claire and Lisa admitted the sad songs had them reaching for the Kleenex, while H, predictably, went mad for the happy bits when everyone was up and dancing. 'We've been compared with them,' remarked Lee, 'but they lasted for over a decade.' It's

Luscious Lisa struts her stuff

Lovely Lee smoulders sexily

Gorgeous Claire hits a high note

Hunky
H goes for
gold

Foxy Faye gets funky

Those dance Steps ...

Shaking their booty in '5-6-7-8'

Striking a pose in 'Last Thing On My Mind'

V for Victory in 'One For Sorrow'

Doing the hairwash in 'Tragedy'

Dancing Queens (and Kings) – The Abba tribute at the 1999 Brit Awards

Driving them wild at Party In The Park

up to Steps to show how long they can last!

WHO'S LIKE STEPS?

Steps are constantly compared with:

BUCKS FIZZ

Two boys and two girls who won Eurovision in 1981 with 'Making Your Mind Up' – a song that gets replayed on what-happened-next type TV quiz shows, because the boys ripped the skirts off the girls in mid-song (*try that on Faye and you'll get a black eye! – Ed*). A re-formed Fizz with just one original member still play the clubs and 1980s nostalgia festivals. One-time Bucks Fizz singer Cheryl Baker went on to become a TV hostess.

BANANARAMA

The story behind this one is the link between Bananarama and Pete Waterman, who took them beyond the Supremes and made them the biggest-selling girl group in British chart history. H was certainly a fan of Siobhan, Keren and Sarah – but, right, no boys! Siobhan married pop's nutty professor Dave Stewart and sang with Shakespears Sister, Keren Woodward got married to George Michael's Wham! partner Andrew Ridgeley, and rumour has it that they're set for a comeback.

ABBA

The Swedish foursome are always compared with Steps – and forever will be now the fab five have done 'Thank Abba For The Music'. Abba sold gazillions of records after their 1974 Eurovision win with 'Waterloo', and ruled the decade with their fabulous Scandinavian pop. It all went wrong after the couples married, and then found they didn't get on. Divorce and a split ended the story in 1983, but the music lives on.

THE BROTHERHOOD OF MAN

Even more ancient Eurovision winners, Brotherhood of Man first charted in 1970. Like Abba, two members of the group ended up as husband and wife (*Claire and Lee, don't even think about it! – only joking, Ed*). They still play the circuit, turning out their mighty 1976 winner 'Save All Your Kisses For Me' as well as a lot of Abba-esque stuff from later in the decade including chart-toppers 'Angelo' and 'Figaro' (shades of 'Chiquitita' and 'Fernando').

KATRINA AND THE WAVES

Faye's faves had been going for yonks before they won Eurovision in 1997 with 'Love Shine A Light'. A boy-girl group, but with lots of the former, they're not so much heard of now Katrina herself has become a Radio 2 DJ and works for TV programmes like *Watchdog*. By the way her surname is Leskanich – reason enough to take an H-like nickname we'd have thought!

SPICE GIRLS

Well, what can we say except that they reduced their numbers from five to four so no-one would compare 'em with the mighty Steps? Okay, they've got no boys in the line-up – but we reckon Lee could beat Beckham in a one-to-one providing it wasn't at Old Trafford in front of 55,000 people. And H has got an initial in his name like Mel C and Mel B, and Lisa's fitter than Sporty, and . . . (*cuuuut! – Ed*).

STEPS ON TRACK

The songs that made their name – we examine the Steps songbook track by pulsating track!

SINGLES

5,6,7,8

Month of release: November 1997
Chart peak: 14
A catchy line-dance thing that would turn out to be nothing like the rest of their repertoire. Lots of 'yee-hah!' potential in a song H says 'nobody liked . . . but everybody bought!'

LAST THING ON MY MIND

Month of release: April 1998
Chart peak: 6
An old Bananarama song, amazingly, that really did the business when given the Steps 1990s makeover. Super turbocharged for dancing.

ONE FOR SORROW

Month of release: August 1998
Chart peak: 2
An up-tempo tear-jerker, if that's possible – and one

with great scope for those distinctive dance floor hand signals!

HEARTBEAT/TRAGEDY (DOUBLE A-SIDE)
Month of release: November 1998
Chart peak: 1
A smart move – a ballad from the album linked with a brand new version of the Bee Gees classic made for a chart-topping combination early in the new year.

BETTER BEST FORGOTTEN
Month of release: March 1999
Chart peak: 2
Fifth and final single from *Step One* – and did they save the best till last? You betcha! This is one you won't forget in a hurry, that's for sure . . .

ALBUM – STEP ONE

Month of release: 14 September 1998
Chart peak: 2
Tracks:
1 Steptro
Kicking off the album and getting in the mood with a storming instrumental was a shrewd move.
2 Last Thing On My Mind
Second single that proved after their first smash that Steps were no one-hit wonders – they're here to stay.
3 5,6,7,8
The song that started it all just had to be on here – and amazingly even the group are beginning to warm to it!
4 One For Sorrow
H's favourite track because of Claire's 'brilliant' vocal performance. A winner all the way, from the Abba-esque intro to the final fade.

5 Heartbeat

The one slushy song (sung by Claire) everyone in Steps has a soft spot for! A single by popular demand, and a Christmas cracker at that!

6 This Heart Will Love Again

An adult theme here explored over a suitably rugged backing: three minutes and 49 seconds of choppy guitar and thunderous drums.

7 Experienced

Boy power rules as H flexes his vocal talents to maximum effect. Rick Astley reborn . . . why haven't we heard this before?

8 Too Weak To Resist

Okay, more manly stuff – what can we say? An eye- and ear-opener for unbelievers, a treat for the rest of us.

9 Better Best Forgotten

Back to familiar territory the moment the girls start hollering over the top of a typical Steps intro. A fine single.

10 Back To You

There's something familiar about this charming ditty that we can't quite put our finger on . . . but we're happy to keep playing the track until we figure it out!

11 Love You More

Lisa and Faye go for this as their standout track because it's clubby and danceable. And who are we to disagree?

12 Stay With Me

A nice downbeat, romantic way to end the album of your dreams. Until you press play once again, that is . . .

Recorded and mixed at PWL Studios in Manchester and London.
Producers:
Topham/Twigg/Waterman (Tracks 1-4, 9, 10)
Frampton/Waterman (Tracks 5,7,8)
Sanders/Frampton/Waterman (Track 6)
Work In Progress (Track 11)
Sanders/Waterman (Track 12)
Musicians:
Keyboards: Steve Parker, Karl Twigg, Mark Topham
Drums: Paul Waterman, Chris McDonnell
Guitar: Mark Topham, Chris Upton, Greg Bone, Dave Williams
Multi-instrumentalists: Andrew Frampton, Dan Sanders
Banjo: Sean Lyons
Violin: Chris Haigh

WHAT THEY SAID ABOUT *STEP ONE*:
'Set to become the pop album of the year.' *Music Week*
'Explicitly magnificent pop.' *Melody Maker*
'I said "Mum, don't buy it! They might beat us!" But she went out and bought it . . .' James Dean Bradfield (Manic Street Preachers) on Radio 1

SIX STUPENDOUS FACTS ABOUT *STEP ONE*:
1 Australian fans will find a bonus track on their version of *Step One* – a remix of 'Last Thing On My Mind'.
2 The cover is even better upside down than the right way up!
3 It was *Live & Kicking* magazine's Album of the Month, and *The Times* Pop Album of the Year.
4 If 'Stay With Me' had been a hit single it would've

been be the eighth different song of that title to chart.

5 *Step One*'s colour scheme, pink and blue, echoes the traditional colours of the sexes: pink for girls and blue for boys.

6 H doesn't think there's a bad track on it!

6a We agree!

DANCE STEPS

The idea of a group that's all-singing and all-dancing isn't a new one – back in the Swinging Sixties, Diana Ross and her Supremes were twirling in time, while a few years before that Cliff Richard, bless him, was doing the hand jive. That's a dance you do with your hands – your grandparents may remember it!

But Steps have clearly brought the pop-dance concept kicking and screaming into the current decade, just in time for the Millennium. And that was always the intention. Their manager Tim Byrne was so convinced that they needed to be seen as well as heard that he wouldn't play interested record companies any tapes of Steps' music. Instead, he kept them rehearsing with choreographer Paul Roberts, who'd worked with All Saints, Clock and Livin' Joy, to get them totally in step with the masterplan. And patience paid off, because the first company to see their performance of '5,6,7,8' couldn't put pen to paper quickly enough!

The revival of dance floor action was certainly timely. With *Grease* and *Saturday Night Fever* both enjoying big revivals on stage as well as screen, the idea of getting on the floor and strutting your stuff was very much the in thing. As for singing as well, that posed problems. The twirling Four Tops and Temptations got round the problems with microphone stands, and would hang up their mikes before indulging in the fancy footwork, but Steps would have none of that. Headset microphones were the answer, and they've since become something of a trademark.

The success of '5,6,7,8' was certainly helped by the line-dancing craze sweeping the country, but some people took the Wild West theme a little too far. When it hit, producer Pete Waterman got phone calls from Nashville, the home of country music, congratulating him on making country a hit in Britain! We're not sure Steps would have seen things like that! 'We were all positive from the start,' explains H, 'even though people tried to dismiss us as line dancers. You always remember those people. Now they've come crawling back and we say "Bye bye"!' Quite right, too.

As H goes on to explain, 'Last Thing On My Mind' deliberately took off in a different direction. 'The theme of the video's the 1970s, and the dance routine's got a touch of that, too. People can pick up on this one really easily, 'cos they're the sort of moves anyone can do.' That's the secret of Steps' success – a little bit of practice plus a lot of imagination and you too can strut like the fab five! H is living proof of that. 'I've never done any training – I learned to dance at the disco!' he shrugs cheerfully.

'Last Thing . . .' introduced a new kind of movement that quickly earned the 'shampooing' label: it looked for all the world as if Steps were washing their hair in the shower! Rounding it all off, though, was the pointing right forefinger as used so often by John Travolta in *Saturday Night Fever*: 'Look at me, I'm a star'. Five stars, more like.

If all that was undeniably impressive, the next routine, for 'One For Sorrow', was considerably more ambitious. While 'Last Thing . . .' had seen everyone performing in unison, this one separated the girls from the boys. As the instrumental section pounded away, the girls held their heads while the boys flailed their arms; then everything snapped back together with a left turn and clap. Just to ensure we all remember, the chorus included the familiar pointing motion, but this time with a twist. The single pointing finger was 'one for sorrow', and the two drawn across the face represented 'two too much'. Unbeatable!

It's an occupational hazard of being a Step that someone, somewhere is bound to expect you to demonstrate one of your dance routines. That can be particularly embarrassing if you're at a party and intent on enjoying yourself. Lisa recalls only too vividly the time she was 'dragged on to the dance floor and made to show the whole club all the moves,' while Lee always makes a beeline for the darkest corner he can find before he's recognized. 'I like to stand back and watch other people enjoying themselves,' he claims modestly.

H is a little less embarrassed, having taught *The Big Breakfast*'s Johnny and Denise to do the '5,6,7,8' dance along with a fascinated Aqua. He's done pretty well really, considering that Faye, Lee and Lisa have all done serious dance training; H and Claire have had to catch on quick. It may take them a little longer, but they're always inch-perfect in the end. The only real disadvantage Claire seems to have in the dancing stakes is her small ears. Why? Because her headphone mike is apt to slip off if she's too energetic! Faye had to face a different problem when she wore her hair in a ponytail at the 1999 Brits. 'I tried to do rehearsals with it,' she explains, 'and it kept whacking people in the face and getting caught under my armpit!'

Dancing the Steps way may be a good way to keep fit and shed pounds, but don't forget to look out for the frogs! Silly boy H has encouraged people to start throwing stuffed frogs on stage, because he collects them. Not that that's the worst thing that can happen. Faye and Lisa have both been victims of a descending skirt when gyrating too quickly for the zipper to stand the strain, but got away with it by smiling and yanking – in that order!

'It was on a TV performance,' says Faye of her 'undie-cover' accident. 'But I was lucky 'cos I had a pair of safety shorts on underneath which were the same colour. The skirt came right down and I didn't even notice . . . but one quick spin and it was done up again.'

Lisa's worst dance floor moment happened before she joined Steps, when she was doing cabaret with two other girls. A smoke machine was leaking water on to the stage, and a greasy compère chap the girls had taken an instant dislike to came out to open the show . . . only to fall flat on his backside! 'I burst out laughing and started saying "What an idiot, ha ha ha",' admits Lisa . . . who went on and, you guessed it, promptly slipped and fell in exactly the same place herself. 'Everyone started laughing at me,' she recalls, admitting she deserved her 'come-uppance'.

Nothing like that happens these days, thank goodness – everything's planned right down to the last movement. Things have got a whole lot more energetic, too – the last tour saw all kinds of gymnastic feats going on, including Lisa taking a ride on H's back! Let's just be glad the smoke machine was behaving itself or there could have been quite an accident . . .

It's not just Steps on stage these days, of course. They're accompanied by five dancers – on the last tour, these were Lizzy Carlin, Shelina Somani, Graham Lloyd, John Shentall and Darren Cornish. Their job is to add a new visual dimension to the performance, sometimes acting out the theme of the songs or giving more interest to the stage goings-on. In 'Stay With Me Tonight', for instance, Faye and Lisa duetted on vocals while a male and a female dancer mimed what the characters would probably be doing in the video had it been a single.

The section of the performance that contains a medley of Disney themes also gives the dancers a chance to strut their stuff. On 'One Jump Ahead' from *Aladdin*, they performed as the characters you'd see in the film's marketplace scene; later, while one of the males carried H on stage on his back, the others paraded proudly in front of him as he sang 'I Just Can't Wait To be King' (from *The Lion King*). Then, as 'Circle Of Life' from the same film ended the medley, they danced along the back of the platform and the steps leading up to it.

But when it comes to the stage show, all eyes are fixed on our famous five. Whether resplendent in those famous matching blue outfits, dressed as Superman, Pocohontas or the Little Mermaid, they're the undisputed centre of attention. And that's the way it should be. Seeing Lee, Lisa, H, Faye and Claire twirling, clapping, pointing and kicking in perfect unison is what it's all about.

Despite the fact that they spend their working days dancing, like all keen students Steps are quite happy to take their work home with them. 'Faye and I are partners in partying,' reveals Lisa. 'If I need someone to go out with, then I'll say to Faye, "Come out and be my partner in crime tonight!"' So if you see two familiar faces arriving at the club you're at, stand by for some fancy footwork!

If it's true that dancing started out as a courtship ritual (oo-er), then surely Steps are the sexiest group around! That's news to encourage Lee, because though Lisa reckons asking people to dance is old-fashioned these days – 'You just dance all together, don't you?' – Lee would quite like to pass on his skills to another group well-known to the charts. 'I had a little boogie with Billie Piper at our album launch party,' he confesses, 'but I'd really like to dance with the Honeyz . . . they're very sexy!'

20 STEPS

Fed up with fascinating facts on your pop heroes and heroines? Thought not! Sit back and prepare to be entertained, big style, by a selection of little-known Steps-type morsels. We think you might just be surprised!

1 When they first visited Australia, Steps did a show at Segaworld, and were amazed to find some very familiar faces in the audience. No surprise really, 'cos the entire cast of hit soap *Home And Away* had come to see them!

2 For legal reasons, Steps weren't allowed to use the word Disney in advertising their stage medley of hit film songs. Don't ask us to explain . . .

3 Faye couldn't visit Japan with the rest of the group in early 1999 because she had a really bad case of the flu. Ah, so . . .

4 The disco-tastic second single 'Last Thing On My Mind' had been a flop for Bananarama in 1992 before Steps revived and revitalised it.

5 Breakthrough track '5,6,7,8' managed to sell 280,000 copies in the UK, even though it never quite made it into the national Top 10!

6 For a bet, Claire once stole a four-foot high sunflower from a hotel in Germany. She folded it

in half, plonked it in a big black suit carrier (to keep your clothes clean) and carried it out over her head!

7 H is addicted to the QVC satellite TV shopping channel. He just loves gadgets such as vacuum cleaners that folds blankets (no, we don't understand it either!).

8 When Claire goes to bed, she snuggles up to a Winnie the Pooh pyjama case that's so realistic it even has a battery-operated heartbeat in it!

9 Faye has been a vegetarian 'on and off' for some time now, and admits that, even though her idea of heaven is eating Marks & Spencers meals every night, she can rustle up 'a dodgy salad' when she absolutely has to.

10 H always winks at the camera when he's on TV, even though he knows it's 'so cheesy!'

11 The first two Steps singles both had ballads as B-sides, to prove there was more than one side to the group.

12 While in Singapore, Lisa and Faye jumped into the hotel swimming pool at midnight to cool themselves down . . . and got caught by the management!

13 Don't forget to brush morning, noon and night – Smiley Step Lisa claims she's never, ever had any fillings whatsoever!

14 *New Musical Express*, the 'alternative rock' paper for the Steve Lamacq generation, amazed everyone by giving a rare rave review to Steps' Croydon show in March 1999. The headline? 'Super Troup!'

15 Amusingly given their current Disney medley, H once refused to dress up as Simba the Lion King at Butlin's. The costume, he explained, was a

total embarrassment, and included something that 'looked like a giant Marigold washing-up glove to put on my head!'

16 One of Steps' fans in Belgium is so keen on the group that she faxes their office every single day, and is there at the airport to meet 'em when they play her country, even at three in the morning!

17 H fancies playing a concert at the Millennium Dome, since one or two members of Steps live 'just around the corner'.

18 Claire first enjoyed a snog in the cinema while 'watching' *The Bodyguard*, starring Kevin Costner and Whitney Houston. Unfortunately for her and her date, they were still 'at it' when the film ended, and had to be asked to leave!

19 Faye keeps two diaries, one for her innermost personal thoughts and another for work stuff. 'My friend saw the secret diary when I was younger,' she blushes, 'so now I hide it well.'

20 H was once so aggravating on a foreign flight that, back on solid ground, the rest of the group tied him up and put him on the never-ending belt of a luggage carousel!

STEPS ON THE ROAD

The show's just about to begin, and all eyes are on the stage. Well, to be exact they're all on the big circular screen hovering over the stage like the spaceship in the blockbusting movie *Independence Day*. Suddenly, an 'alien voice' start talking to us. 'Scream if you want Steps!' it says, then 'Louder!' Sorry, that should be 'LOUDER!', 'cos everything's in capitals on this screen to help those at the back to see what's going on. Finally comes 'WE CAN'T HEAR YOU', at which point the decibel count goes through the roof like a space shuttle blasting off.

A video then replaces the words, showing what's supposed to be going on in the two backstage dressing rooms. Lisa, Faye and Claire are carefully attending to their make-up, while H and Lee squeeze their muscles and pose with footballs. This gets a particularly loud cheer! Then the lights go down, the stage is illuminated and five brightly dressed creatures bound on to start the show.

But hang on a mo. The ninety-odd minutes which the audience gets to see is just the tip of a big, big iceberg. A small army is employed to make sure the show goes off smoothly each and every night, and this backroom team is every bit as important as the five characters the public see.

John, the road manager, has the most difficult task – to make sure everyone is exactly where they should be at the appointed time, the stage is properly set up, and everything backstage is hunky-dory. In fact, John is there to oil the wheels of the tour and to ensure that everything runs super-smoothly. As you might imagine, he's worked with a whole range of different acts during his career, so when he says Steps are 'in many ways the easiest band I've worked with' it's quite a compliment! He thinks the show is different, 'like pantomime', and confesses to having a little boogie at the side of the stage when everything's going to plan.

The caterers ensure everyone, from coach drivers to roadies, get fed and watered when they need to be. Everything from breakfast and lunch to a posh three-course dinner can be supplied, though they say Steps are fond of plain food like jacket potatoes and beans on toast. Lisa, in particular, is none too keen on foreign food, so will order her old standby, sausage and chips, if she can't find anything she likes the look of.

The sound is dealt with by Mark, whose official title is Front of House Sound Engineer. That means he has control of what we hear in the audience, balancing the volumes of vocals, instruments and effects so that Steps live sound just as good as – if not better than – the records! Someone else at the venue will feed the sound back to the group who, instead of the usual wedge-shaped monitor speakers rock bands have used since the dawn of time, have state of the art personal earpieces.

The idea of Steps' show being like a pantomime is spot-on. Aside from the numerous costume changes, there's laughter, music, visuals, dancing and tremendous all-round entertainment. You'd think a group who had only done one album – amazing though it is – might come up short of material. No such problem with Steps – in fact they've got so many ideas that the occasional album track, like 'Back To You', just couldn't be squeezed into the running order. Instead, an amazing version of 'I'll Be There For You' (the Rembrandts' theme from the hit US TV show *Friends*, as if you really needed reminding) jostled for attention with the stunning medley of characters and songs from Disney films.

Someone once said that when you're a star you're never off duty. That's something Steps called to mind when they arrived at a hotel after what Claire described as a 'zillion-hour flight' to find limousines, maids and flunkies carrying bouquets. 'I said, "Guys, someone really important must just have arrived." So we all had our faces pressed up against the window of the bus, the doors opened and we all fell out . . .' Of course, the welcoming committee was for them. 'And there we were,' complains Faye, 'sprawled on the floor in our hats and sunglasses!'

Hotel stays are always fun for Steps, especially as they've now adopted the time-honoured rock'n'roll tactic of signing in under daft names. Apart from winding up the desk clerk, this also has the desirable side-effect of making sure fans can't track down our famous five and start banging on their doors in the middle of the night! In case you're interested in doing just that, girls, we can exclusively reveal that H has been known in his time as Mr G String, and Lee as Mr A Cappella.

Happily, the days of Steps members sharing rooms have long gone, and each lad and lass now has their own space. With five different habits and sleeping patterns, it was not a moment too soon. H and Lisa, the well-known messy Steps, could have enough room to fling all their stuff about. 'H always ends up sleeping on my lap in the tour bus,' complains Claire, 'even though I hate it!' Mind you, he's worse on planes! H isn't the world's greatest traveller, and has been known to express his displeasure if any aeroplane Steps are in should encounter air turbulence. He also likes to be at the back of the plane 'in case there are any spare seats to stretch out on!'

Long before Steps even think of setting foot on stage, they'll be in promotion mode – visiting radio stations, signing CDs in record stores, cheering up sick children in hospital or doing something else to spread the word. Any other time they have to themselves can be spent resting or shopping – in disguise, naturally!

The moments before curtain-up are always the scariest for any group, and Steps are no exception. The girls do vocal exercises to warm up their voices, and just before they go on the five go into a rugby scrum-like huddle with their dancers. It's a habit they've borrowed from American sport, Claire explains. 'Then we put our hands in the middle and shout at the top of our voices!'

The audiences Steps have played to have varied from college crowds – where they start out having to impress the audience and end up being cheered to the rafters by sozzled students – to town halls full of young fans with their big sisters and mothers. Arena dates set up for late 1999 will bring more new challenges.

Special memories so far include a roadshow in a big outdoor tent in Swansea, where the whole place was flooded. 'By the time we went on stage,' Faye recalls, 'there was no one there!' They were top of the bill, and having been entertained by many other acts the crowd had got restless and made tracks for home. When Steps did get on, the electricity blew so they had to get off stage again. Finally, as the group performed to a small but select audience, a lightning flash came perilously close to them. 'Luckily,' laughs Lee, 'it was at the end of a song, so it looked as if it was meant to happen!'

After the show, it's time to have fun. All the Steps are party people, so there's little chance they'll hot-foot it back to their bedrooms when they come off stage. If time allows they'll take in the resident cabaret – at one hotel in Scarborough the band did a version of 'Tragedy' in their honour!

Sometimes the unpredictable happens and Steps actually have a day off! It's such a rare occurrence – you could forgive them for falling over in a faint when it happens – but when it happened in the seaside town of Scarborough they decided to go out on the town as a fivesome. Off they went for a fish and chip supper, after which they manned the lanes for a spot of ten-pin bowling. When that finished at ten, they headed back to their hotel for a nightcap in the bar, and were all in bed by half-past eleven. Phew, rock'n'roll!

Working as hard as Steps do means they have to look after their health – after all, the chain is only as strong as its weakest link, and if one Step should be missed then the show just can't go on! H is one for his vitamin tablets, and claims his life is a round of 'saunas, jacuzzis and early nights'. Lee breakfasts on grapefruit and yoghurt (ugh!), and never eats much late at night as it upsets his stomach. He's more likely to be calling room service for cereal at any time of the day or night, claiming 'it's light and never bloats you.' So if you're wondering who puts the snap, crackle and pop in Steps, look no further!

With groups like Steps, demand for tickets always outstrips supply – which means unless your parents have their credit card at the ready you'll have to move fast to see them. So many people were disappointed when Steps played their first nationwide tour in the spring of 1999 that the Next Step arena tour was already being advertised as the last notes of the final show were fading into the distance. This time around, theatres were giving way to huge venues like the Sheffield Arena, Birmingham NEC, the Cardiff International Arena (a home gig for H and Lisa) and the Manchester Evening News Arena. All this meant that even more people could share in the Steps experience. And for anyone who's into the Internet, fans could even order their tickets on-line!

Steps now have touring down to a fine art. Their tour bus comes equipped with no fewer than three big television sets on which to watch programmes or videos, while the blokes are always to be found playing on the Sony Playstation. We can't count the number of times H and Lee have done battle on Porsche Challenge, though Lee claims he should play for money because he can beat all-comers. There's always a football on board too in case a flat patch of grass presents itself.

H has developed an interest in books, which is a first – after watching the Tom Cruise/Brad Pitt *Interview With The Vampire* film he started reading the Anne Rice novel, and now has a horror novel fetish. It's when he starts eating raw meat you have to worry! He still remembers the time he was stranded outside the tour bus when they drove off without him, so you won't find H setting foot on the tarmac alone. When he's allowed out in company for a look around he hunts for toy shops where they might sell Steiff teddy bears, his latest collecting craze (after frogs, since you ask!).

Touring abroad presents its own challenges, not least of which is the language. If you're looking for someone to help you learn the lingo, then don't ask H! 'It's funny,' says Lisa. 'When we're abroad I always learn practical phrases like "Where is the bus stop?", while H finds out all the rude words!' No such language problem in Australia, a country which has particularly taken to Steps. They've always found a warm welcome waiting Down Under, and have even given their fans there the occasional bonus remix on their releases to keep them happy.

Wherever they are in the world, Steps on the road are a group like no other. They once tried to live the rock'n'roll lifestyle and trash a room, but were so shocked with what they'd done that they put everything back together immediately! 'I think the place was in a better state when we left the hotel than it was when we first got there,' laughs Lee. Recently he's been staying in rooms which feature two king-size beds – and he hasn't even had to share. Now that's pop stardom for ya! But the problem for Claire is how to bring back all her souvenirs – last time she went to America she had to buy a new suitcase to cram everything in!

So next time you're waiting in anticipation for Steps to arrive on stage, don't forget everything that's gone on to get them there for you. Enjoy the show – and remember, SCREAM IF YOU WANT STEPS!

STEPS WORLD-WIDE

'Eurovision' they may be, according to some people, but in the two years or so they've been together Steps have conquered more than just the European Community – they're a worldwide phenomenon! Music lovers across the globe have voted with their feet, dancing the night away to Steps' album and singles, proving that when you produce music this good it doesn't matter where you come from! And that's enough to get our vote . . .

Whisper it quietly, but *Step One* was actually released in Australia a month ahead of Britain – so you can excuse the fans Down Under if they consider Faye, H, Lee, Lisa and Claire to be five of their own. It gave Steps a chance to promote the album over there without neglecting their home audience, and it was no surprise when the album shot up to Number 7 in the land of kangaroos and Kylie.

With Steps there to promote it in person the first single '5,6,7,8' made it right to the top in Oz, while closer to home 'Last Thing On My Mind' gave them a Top 20 place in Sweden and Holland. Belgium sent it straight to the top and has proved a Steps stronghold ever since, which pleases the guys and girls 'cos when they make frequent flying visits they get to bring back loads of that country's most famous export – chocolate!

The Far East is another region where Steps-mania has taken hold. Boy bands may be big there, but Steps are even bigger! The album went platinum in the Philippines and gold in Taiwan and Hong Kong, while Malaysia gave them such a welcome that Claire rated it best of all the countries they've visited in those parts. Having spent some time out there, Lee and Lisa like Eastern cuisine, but the other three aren't quite so adventurous. 'If I don't like the look of it,' says H with a determined look on his face, 'I won't go near it.' So, another McDonald's, then, Mr Watkins?

So eager were they to make friends with their Eastern audience that Steps agreed when they released '5,6,7,8' to each learn a line in a different language to impress the locals. Difficult, eh? Now multiply by the five Asian countries they visited and it's nothing short of a tongue-twister. 'If it's Tuesday, it must be Singapore . . . Doh! I've forgotten the words!'

Steps are better equipped than most when it comes to travelling. Everything from pillows to jammies (Lisa's, natch), Game Boys to Walkmen are now listed, laundered and packed automatically by the tour manager and his team. Our heroes don't have to lift a finger – because even though this group's called Steps their feet rarely touch the ground! Back in Britain it's all aboard their luxurious tour bus, which is equipped with every possible need and more besides. Some would call it a hotel on wheels . . .

Things have been so busy for the hard-working fivesome that Lee admits sometimes 'we didn't know who we were, where we were and why we were there!' The quote came at the end of their hardest-working week to date, when they flew back from sunny Cuba (where they'd just filmed the video for 'Last Thing On My Mind') only to stop off in Spain for a personal appearance on the way home. Then, after a full twelve hours in Blighty, they were on their way again to Sweden before returning to that pile of dirty washing on the kitchen floor . . . via Belgium!

Thankfully that was an extreme week, but when you hear that Steps had to make an eighteen-hour flight to Australia straight after twelve solid hours rehearsing and performing, you begin to wonder who draws up their timetable! On the other hand, Lisa and Faye felt so wide-awake once they'd arrived Down Under they immediately headed for the nearest nightclub. Needless to say, it was dark glasses for both ladies next morning!

There's occasionally the chance to go shopping in these exotic countries, and, though the girls run him close, H reckons he can beat anyone when it comes to letting loose those travellers' cheques. His record is £1,500 in half an hour in Singapore. If you think you can do better, we pity your poor credit card! Lee thinks quality not quantity, though rumours he's a stingy northerner who stashes his cash under the bed are total lies . . . well, Lee says so anyway!

Steps have left their mark on a few hotels in the past, though, being charming and polite, unlike many pop groups, it's only been in the guest book! Their all-time favourite establishment is one in Belgium that looks like a castle, but anywhere they go these days is pretty luxurious considering they no longer have to share rooms. Look out, though, if you find yourself sharing their hotel – they used to strip H naked and send him down in a lift! What was that we were saying about being charming and polite . . .?

One problem about hotels wherever you are in the world is remembering exactly where they are. Poor old H decided to go for a walk in the garden of the hotel when Steps were staying in Japan, then ventured a little further afield to a gift shop. He came out with his pressies, turned in the wrong direction and, on getting back to the hotel, found it was a completely different one to the one he'd started out from! Embarrassing or what?

No matter what language is spoken, once Steps get on television and start showing off their fancy footwork a hit is the inevitable result. They've proved their music is an international language, and there's little doubt that when it comes to uniting Europe, if not the world, these five have more pulling power than politicians, football stars or anyone else you care to name. Move over Manchester United – Steps Rule the World!

POP STAR PALS

Pop stars tend to like the company of pop stars – it's crazy, but true! Just look at Rich and Billie, Robbie and Nicole, Sonny and Cher (ask your mum!) . . . the list goes on. Why should this be? Well, only people who've had first-hand experience of living their life in pop's goldfish bowl can understand what it's like. Also, when you've time on your hands hanging round at festivals, radio stations or *Top Of The Pops*, you tend to run into the same people again and again.

So it's no surprise that Steps' address books are full of the numbers of famous friends. Lee's got Spike Dawbarn's number programmed on his mobile phone, because he went to college with the 911 singer, and also Rich Five, whom he's met quite a few times on pop shows all over the world. They can keep each other up to date on what's going on in various parts of the world, and exchange tips on shops to visit or TV shows to avoid.

Spike once played a rather nasty trick on Lee, removing his clothes from where they'd been left a heap in the bathroom when he was having a shower. 'When I came out,' Lee recalls, 'all that was left was a shoe on the window ledge. Spike was in the studio and I had to make my way there to retrieve them, with my hands placed in an awkward position. I'll get my revenge . . .' With pals like that, who needs enemies?

Pop friends can sometimes help you out of sticky situations. Take Claire and Saffron from Republica. 'She passed me some toilet paper in the loo!' Ms Richards confesses. 'I didn't know it was her, but then I came out and they were all going "That was Thingy from Republica!" I was, "Oh, wow, Saffron passed me bog roll!"' Could be the start of a long, strong and very absorbing friendship!

If the news that pop stars use the loo too comes as something of a shock, then the nervous among you should skip the next bit – Lisa insists that Steps aren't 'pop stars' at all but 'performers'. She can relate to her contemporaries as people, even though childhood heroes and heroines stay up on their pedestals. Having started off around the same time as Five and Cleopatra, she sees them as friends – 'whereas people like Madonna will always be stars to me.'

H is still very much a pop fan at heart, bless him, and can't help introducing himself to any star in the vicinity – particularly if they're female! Take the time that he first met special favourites Cleopatra. 'I told Lee I was going to be cool,' he revealed, 'but I waved and shouted "Hi", so I wasn't cool at all.' Luckily Cleo waved back (think how embarrassing it would have been if they hadn't!) so all was well. 'I asked Lee later if I'd been cool,' concludes H, 'and he said "As cool as you'll ever be, mate!"'

Lee admits he 'just tends to say hello to people, no matter who they are or what they do. I even said to Meatloaf, "Hello mate, how are you doing?" Perhaps if it was some mega film star or something I would, but for some reason I don't get star-struck with pop stars.'

So if you see Lee out and about, don't be shy – he certainly isn't.

Claire recalls an example of Lee's habit of asking everyone for their number. 'We bumped into B*Witched in a motorway service station, and he said "Don't think I'm being funny or anything, but can I have your numbers and then we can have a chat now and again?"'

Mind you, Claire would be the first to admit that friends in high places can help open doors. When she was in her first serious group TSD, she toured with that dynamic Newcastle duo Ant and Dec, then in pop star mode as PJ and Duncan. They got along famously, and early 1999 saw the dynamic duo renewing the acquaintance when they invited her back to be a guest star on their weekend SMTV show.

Claire was officially there to cover for the holidaying Cat Deeley, but we reckon she did so well there's a TV hostess in her just waiting to get out! Ant revealed that Claire had only an hour and a half to read the scripts, but 'she was brilliant!' Dec praised her 'lovely personality', before marvelling at the fact that 'she managed to walk and talk at the same time – and that's not easy!' Claire, for her part, claims that even though she's performed in concert in front of thousands, appearing on live TV made her 'so nervous! The worst bit was CD:UK because that was really live . . . no rehearsals at all. I think Cat's job is safe, but I'd definitely do it again. I loved every minute of it!'

Steps are always aware that while they're at the top of the showbiz pile there are a lot of people still on their way up. So any act lucky enough to be chosen to open a Steps show can be certain of a good reception from the headliners as well as from the audience!

Christian Fry, A1 and Lolly were the special guests on their Step One tour, and soon became part of the Steps gang. Party animal Christian clicked immediately with Faye and Lisa, the two Steps for whom the fun never stops, while H is a huge fan of Lolly. He even came out occasionally to dance alongside her as she gave her all in a spirited version of the 1980s hit 'Mickey'. Great stuff!

The same happened when *TV Hits* magazine ran a competition for people to dance with Steps. The three winners, Gemma, Sara and Natalie from Sheffield, were whisked down to London to show the guys their routine for 'Better Best Forgotten' which had wowed their school assembly. Because there was no stereo in the hotel room, Steps sang the song together *a cappella* (unaccompanied) for the trio to perform to, which Gemma later admitted was 'like having our own private Steps concert'. With Faye acting as dinner lady and dishing out the sarnies and drinks, the overall impression was that 'they were so nice, not like pop stars at all.' So if these three Sheffield lasses ever make their name as pop stars, Steps can take the credit for encouragement when they started off.

If meeting that trio from Sheffield was a bit of a 'girl thing', Claire enjoyed another female frolic in the company of Billie, B*Witched and Cleopatra when the groups teamed up in early 1999 for their Abba tribute. After rehearsals they planned to go out clubbing to let off steam, but she soon found a flaw in the plan: 'Billie and Cleo wouldn't be let in!' No such problems for Bjorn Ulvaeus, the guy from Abba who doesn't have a beard – the group met him at the premiere of *Mamma Mia*, and have bumped into him a few times since. 'He's getting to be a bit of a mate these days.'

Despite all his pop star pals, H admits he still gets

nervous when he meets famous people. As for going out with one, the thought simply scares him stiff! 'I want to ask them for their autograph rather than snog them.' He's certainly got eyes for Louise and Denise Van Outen, but they're both spoken for. So maybe we should turn our eyes to the emerald isle. 'We get on so well with B*Witched. Edele is lovely, she always gives me a big kiss every time I see her . . .'

When it comes to having famous fans, Steps are well up there with the best. Shane Lynch from Boyzone and ex-Take Thatter Mark Owen were among those to drop in and admire their tour. Shane saw them in Manchester, possibly inspired to go by his sisters, and his report on the gig was 'So Good' (sorry!) that Stephen Gately turned up at another show. He requested a couple of signed singles for his collection, and Steps were happy to oblige. The Beautiful South have also been spied in the stalls, while George Michael, no less, wanted to take in the show – unfortunately, every ticket in the house was sold out! Better luck next time, George.

They may be well connected within the show-business world, but Steps haven't deserted the people they knew on the way up – far from it! If you've known someone for years, then you can depend on what they tell you and that's a sure way of making sure you're not getting too big for your boots! On the other hand, Lee needs the reassurance of a friend telling him he's okay. 'This profession brings out people's insecurities,' he explains. 'I used to be the most confident person you could ever meet, but this business can affect you and you have to build yourself up again.'

There's girl friends and there's girlfriends. H recalls sending a girl on his street a heart-shaped lump of bath gel all wrapped up in pretty paper and getting nowhere. 'It was okay, though, because Donna ended up being one of my good friends through school.' He has another friend who happened to be a girl – Billie, no relation to the famous popstrel – and keeps in close touch with her. In fact, he's been asked to 'give her away' at her wedding! He's also a godfather, to a little lad called Ethan. All in all, H's postcard list when Steps visit exotic places like Japan must be amazing!

Ask Lee who his best friend in the world is and it's a guy from home called George. 'We tell each other everything and are always there for each other.' Aaaah! As for his worst enemy, that's just as easy to answer – himself! 'I'm so much harder on myself than anyone could ever be,' he confesses.

Being a pop star is a good way to impress your mates – well, sometimes! Faye had just appeared on *The Big Breakfast* when she was on the mobile for a chat. Her pal said 'I never knew you appeared in the Johnny and Denise video', and Faye was able to say 'Yeah, Denise is standing over there in her Hello Kitty T-shirt'! Her pal hadn't realized she was famous, too, so she clearly hadn't been tuned in that morning!

Sometimes a Step's best friend is her mum. It was certainly that way when Claire's first group TSD got dropped by their record company. It was Mrs Richards' shoulder that got wet that day, but it was also her insistence that her daughter keep following her musical ambitions that brought Claire back from the typing pool. And when her Dad walked her down the 'aisle' in the 'Tragedy' video it was clear that her parents' faith had paid off.

Spending so much time in their own company, maybe it's a good thing that Steps' best friends are each other! They fall out occasionally, of course – H admits that both Faye and Claire have given him a slap on the occasions he's deserved it! – but for the most part they get along just fine. As for whether Lee and Claire have ever been more than friends – that's for you to ask and them to know!

But when pop stars get together, they like nothing more than doing what we all do. At the Brit Awards, H and Boyzone's Stephen Gately could be found in a corner, playing Nintendo and chatting away. 'We get on really well,' revealed H, adding 'He likes singing and dancing but he likes to shy away from the fame thing, and I do too. I'd much rather stay out of the limelight.' We believed it all until that last bit! But let's give master Watkins the final word. 'When you're famous you don't change but the people around you do . . .' That's why it's important to have true friends.

STEPS IN THE STARS

LISA

SCORPIO (BORN 5 NOVEMBER)

Scorpios are highly ambitious, and this fits with Lisa's career path so far. She'll stop at nothing to achieve her goals, and once she's got them she simply will not 'step' aside. Those born under the scorpion are fairly free with their emotions too when it suits them, so Lisa won't suffer fools gladly. If you don't live up to her expectations, prepare for the big E . . . and fast!

Scorpios know no fear and can quite often do silly things out of bravado. Any prospective partner has to be able to minimize this risk without coming over all 'wet' and soppy . . . if the Scorpio thinks this, then all well-meaning advice will be promptly disregarded! Lisa will listen to people she knows and trusts, but is unlikely to take advice from other quarters. She is, however, very loyal – another Scorpio trait – so once you've got her ear you can whisper into it forever!

The privacy-hungry Scorpio can often react badly to the attentions of the press, and will often employ disguises – rock star shades, wigs, etc – to keep unwelcome attentions at bay. But Scorpios are warm-blooded too, and aren't known for hiding themselves away. That means there's a power struggle going on inside the Scorpio's head between the private individual and the public exhibitionist.

Scorpios will travel to the ends of the Earth to reach their goal, and Lisa had a variety of jobs, from burger-bar cook to cabaret queen, before finally achieving fame as one fifth of Steps. Her desire to live in Australia may be a joke now, but don't be surprised to see her making for exotic parts in a permanent way later in life. Maybe she'll marry a foreigner! But there's much more for her to achieve before then, and the only thing that can stop her is herself. Scorpios can lose the plot and get distracted from the job in hand, but as long as she buckles down and tackles her tasks in order of priority, we can't see her failing!

OTHER FAMOUS SCORPIOS

Simon Le Bon (Duran Duran), Dr George Carey (Archbishop of Canterbury), Alex James (Blur), Frank Bruno, Griff Rhys Jones, Jodie Foster

LEE

AQUARIUS (BORN 28 JANUARY)

Aquarians are friendly and outgoing, and have a real interest in others. So if you hook one, you'll find them very into what you're doing. However, they can also overlook the fact that you might not share all their likes and habits, so it can often mean compromise if they whisk you off on a day-trip you'd rather avoid. They're also reluctant to commit themselves, so you have to hope that 'just good friends' means rather more. Don't expect them to start coming over all mushy . . . at least not at first!

Freedom of choice is important for Aquarians, so if you want them to do something, make them think it's their idea, not yours. Aquarius is a water sign, which traditionally could be a bit of a risk for a group. Most Aquarian pop stars seem to prefer working alone, or like Robbie Williams (Take That) and Phil Collins (Genesis) leave to seek solo fame. Lee may yet take that route . . . but we feel he's a long way from breaking free just yet.

As a member of Steps, Lee has to adhere to all kinds of timetables and itineraries, and there are often times when as an Aquarian he'd like to cut loose and go his own way. But that's not possible, so he has to curb his individuality for the good of the others. Being a team player is something he learned as a youth footballer, so it comes more easily to him now.

When it comes to buying Aquarians presents, anything trashy or gimmicky is right up their street. Doesn't matter if it costs a king's ransom or one pound fifty, if it captures their imagination it's good enough. Even impractical presents can strike a chord. Lee's bought some strange things for himself in the past, but he's settled down a lot now.

When it comes to finding a partner, Aquarians and Geminis are made for each other, both physically and mentally. However, Aquarians should avoid Cancerians, who they will see as wanting to tie them down and restrict their ambitions.

OTHER FAMOUS AQUARIANS

Matt Dillon, Mark Owen, Robbie Williams, Vic Reeves, Seal, Bobby Brown, Phil Collins

FAYE

SCORPIO (BORN 14 NOVEMBER)

Those born under the sign of Scorpio are apt to follow their hearts and don't always think about the consequences. Yet they are never going to be happy if they're paraded as 'catches', so if you're looking for a celebrity girlfriend then Faye is not, repeat not, the one for you!

Scorpios are always the last to leave the party, and that's something Faye certainly identifies with! It takes something very special to prise a Scorpio away from the dance floor. In many ways Steps has been a non-stop party for Faye, and that's certainly helped her stick with the work schedule that's never been less than demanding. Scorpios can 'turn off' just like that if their interest isn't captured, so thankfully being in Steps has so far kept her challenged every inch of the way.

Faye shares her birth sign with another member of Steps, of course – and she's already noticed the similarities! 'Lisa and I are both Scorpios and when we both had a day off recently we both did exactly the same things in the same places.' The pair get on too well to fall out as long as they don't both set their sights on the same thing. If it's a bloke, look out for sparks flying in the short term at least – but true Scorpios would never let romance come in the way of a good, strong, solid friendship.

Scorpio's ideal partner is a Cancerian (Tom Cruise, say), because he would be sensitive to her fiery nature but still be strong enough to wear the trousers, so to speak. The men to avoid for Scorpios are Taureans, because they tend to be too down to earth and won't let Scorpios indulge their ambitions and fantasies.

OTHER FAMOUS SCORPIOS

Julia Roberts, Winona Ryder, Prince Charles, Jonathan Ross, Bryan Adams, Larry Mullen (U2), Goldie Hawn, Boris Becker

H

TAURUS (BORN 8 MAY)

Stating the obvious first, those born under the sign of the bull shouldn't go near china shops! H certainly qualifies as the kind of bloke who rushes in where other signs fear to tread. His appetites for everything – food, drink, affection, love – are considerable, and unless you're prepared to dedicate your life to helping him satisfy them then don't even consider entering the farmyard! If you do click, though, put a ring through his nose and you'll be able to lead him anywhere!

Taureans always likes to know where they're going, and if they can't see a future in something they will be unwilling to take that road. H has got round the uncertainties of a pop career by inventing his own little 'H World' where everything turns out all right, every Steps single gets to Number 1 and all his ambitions are attainable. If he ever left showbusiness, he might consider taking up the art career he was set to go into had show-biz not intervened. Certainly, anything that gives creative satisfaction and clear road to future success would satisfy a typical Taurean.

Taurean males love to prove their masculinity by building a dream home which they can live in with their chosen mate. Conservatories, garden sheds, double glazing . . . coming right up, as the bull starts bulldozing! Conversely, they aren't that keen on seeing other people involved, so if you like taking a back seat and letting others do the work, then the Taurus male is for you!

Taurus people should certainly avoid Scorpios. There's far too much suspicion and paranoia lurking there, and straight-talking Taureans just don't want to go there – ever. Put these two in a room and look out for low-flying missiles! On the other hand, Taurus and Libra is a match made in heaven if ever there was one. A good time will be had by all when these two fun-loving signs get together on a date; just don't ask to see the credit card slips afterwards!

FAMOUS TAUREANS

HM the Queen, Bono (U2), Cher, Howard Donald (ex-Take That), Janet Jackson, Robert Smith (The Cure), Al Pacino, Pierce '007' Brosnan

CLAIRE

VIRGO (BORN 17 SEPTEMBER)

Organized? Talk about organized! The average Virgoan has Filofaxes, Palm Pilots, diaries and calendars bulging from every pocket. Ask Claire and she can probably tell you where, when and with whom she's going to be for the next six . . . make that twelve months. Trouble is, you've got to persuade her to make some room in there for you!

Virgos can be a little bit prudish, so Claire's happy Steps now have more than one dressing room in which to get ready – she's not about to show her bits to all and sundry! She's also similar to others of her sign in not wanting to be hurried. She knows the schedule, thank you very much, and she won't be rushed. When TSD folded, Claire went back to a nine-to-five life and ignored any ideas of pop stardom completely. Virgos like things to be cut and dried, but when the chance to come back was offered she grabbed it – after a push from Mum!

Health looms large in any self-respecting Virgoan's life, so expect Claire to start shovelling vitamin pills down your throat if she thinks you're not looking after yourself. And as a Virgo person can be a bit of a control freak, you might soon find your life being run along similar lines. If and when Steps have run their course, you can expect Claire to go into management, advising others and giving them the benefit of her extensive experience.

Virgos' ideal partners are Capricorns, who share their obsession with being absolutely perfect! They can examine their split ends together. But don't put Virgos together with Pisces. They'd run a mile from the highly organized Virgoan and their 'To-Do' lists'!

OTHER FAMOUS VIRGOS

Sean '007' Connery, Keanu Reeves, Lenny Henry, Michael Jackson, Jason Priestley, Charlie Sheen, Bruce Springsteen, Gloria Estefan

STEPS IN LOVE

Steps' five faces gaze down from bedroom walls the world over, from Manchester to Melbourne – and everyone has their favourite. Girls want to mother H or dance the night away with Lee, while lads would love to boogie on down with Lisa – Party Steps herself! – enjoy a romantic dinner with Claire or compare trainers with the ever-approachable Faye. And why not?

The silly thing is that, while all five Steps are friendly and down to earth, with no 'superstar attitude' round their necks, the hectic schedule of pop stardom means that relationships remain just a hazy dream on the horizon. As Lee puts it, 'I do tend to fret a bit when I'm in a new relationship. I wonder where she is and what she's doing.' Add on several thousand miles and you've got some idea of the difficulties involved! How could you leave someone at home for weeks at a time, running up huge phone bills from the other side of the world? It just wouldn't be fair.

Still, the press are always eager to sell newspapers – and if you ask Lee that one annoying question, there will be only one answer: '"Is there any romance in the group?" We get that all the time because Steps are the only mixed group out there who are successful at the moment. There couldn't be, otherwise we wouldn't have got as far as we have.' A fair point, but when three females and two males spend week after week in each other's company, isn't something going to happen?

That was certainly what Britain's top tabloid, *The Sun*, was claiming as 1999 dawned and a sensational story hit their pages. 'Two Steps to Heaven – Secret dates for Claire and Lee' screamed the headline. An 'exclusive' article claimed the romance blossomed during the filming of the 'Tragedy' video, and that the pair had been secretly spending their days off together. 'They have very strong feelings for each other, but were afraid to say anything,' said an anonymous 'group insider'. 'They didn't even tell the three other members of the band. Claire and Lee have tried to be very discreet but they realised they wouldn't be able to keep their relationship a secret for ever.'

A spokesman said 'We knew nothing about the relationship until you told us. When I confronted them they were like a couple of embarrassed, giggling teenagers.' Needless to say, the 'group insider' and 'spokesman' were never given names, and nothing was ever proved about the story. *The Sun* moved on to other 'targets', including Royal bride-to-be Sophie Rhys-Jones, so we'd keep those topless beach snaps under lock and key if we were you, Faye!

It's hard when you're famous to know whether the people you meet are interested in you or your pop star image. According to Lee, Lisa and Faye are the Steps who get chatted up by complete strangers all the time, 'because they're quite good at the whole flirting game', whereas Claire isn't.

It must be tempting if you're a Step to enjoy the occasional, 'holiday romance' as you pass through different parts of the world, but Lee is very much against one-night stands, insisting 'I usually like to get to know the girl first . . . it always ends up building into a relationship because I know the person and like them.' According to Claire, he always plays it cool. 'Lee pulls the girls a lot, but he always waits for them to come to him, so he acts a bit cooler.'

Lee reckons he's only had about four girlfriends in his whole life. He started when he was 12 and has always gone in for long relationships. He's not attached at the moment, which makes things a little unusual for him. Love, he believes, makes you 'feel like you're on cloud nine – you always want to see them, you can't bear to say goodbye and when you get home you're always on the phone.' He's also aware, though, that it can make you overlook other people, especially friends, who are very important. So if Cupid's arrow strikes again, he's going to keep it all very much in perspective. On paper, at least!

Lisa claims that while she's cared for certain young men in her time, she's never actually been 'in love' – she's in love with her job which she admits is 'really sad'. But she's still young . . . H has never known real heartbreak, and there's a very good reason for this – he's never had a long-term relationship! 'I guess I'd like to fall in love some day,' he admits sadly, but the life of a pop star isn't exactly known for making relationships easy. Anyone who fancies making H happy will have to have a well-developed sense of humour. 'H is great when you're feeling down, not that we are very often,' says Lisa. 'If you want a good laugh, go to H.'

While Lisa's busy giving away her pals' love

secrets (*tsk! tsk! – Ed*), she also lets slip that 'Claire falls in love the easiest, 'cos she likes nice things and she's very big-hearted!' But ask Claire herself and she'll admit she finds it hard to put romantic feelings into words. 'I let things go quite a lot, bottle things up.' She admits she's really fussy when it comes to men – she even claims she chucked one ex because she didn't like his jacket! 'If it isn't working, I end it' is her motto when it comes to men, but in the next breath she admits she's still on the lookout for Mr Right. She says she's not bothered about blokes in her past who might kiss and tell, because she hasn't been out with anyone long enough. 'The worst anyone could say is that I never rang them back . . .'

They say the best place to find love is a launderette or a supermarket, but most famous pop stars get someone else to handle those unmentionably boring chores. Steps, though, are nothing if not approachable! 'Once I was out shopping with my mum,' reveals Claire, 'and this boy who must have been twelve or thirteen gave me his phone number. He was a bit too young for me.'

H is certainly feeling the strain of living the pop star life with no one special to confide in. 'I haven't had a relationship for years,' he moans. 'It's not through choice. I haven't had a relationship since this job began, and I can imagine how hard it would be.' Even so, he's willing to give it a go. 'If the right person came along, and they were understanding, let's go for it. Answers on a postcard, please . . .'

When you're a star, you have to make sure you don't get involved with anyone who, if the opportunity presented itself, would do a tabloid 'kiss and tell'. It's certainly something Lisa's aware of. 'I've spoken to some of my ex-boyfriends about it,' she admits. 'They've all assured me they wouldn't do anything like that and I'd like to believe them. They say that if anyone approached them they'd just say what a nice girl I am.'

Unfortunately, since she came up with that assessment, a boy called Andy she'd been going out with for about a year spilt the beans to a tabloid newspaper. Apparently he was heartbroken at Lisa ending their relationship, but if he's the kind of bloke who'd expose their love affair in print he's probably 'Better Best Forgotten'!

LISA LIKES

- David Beckham
- 'Anyone tall and dark who can make me laugh.'
- 'Strong men, tall and dark like Robbie Williams.'

H LIKES

- Cindy Crawford, Denise Van Outen, Louise, B*Witched . . . the list goes on!
- Girls with a sense of humour who won't mind if he burps or breaks wind!

FAYE LIKES

- Leonardo DiCaprio (he's her dream bloke!): 'He's younger than me, but I could handle that!' Before that it was Mark Owen: 'I used to have dreams about him all the time.'
- Someone with a sense of humour who likes picnics and bouncing on beds (!).
- Men in uniform!

LEE LIKES

- Salma Hayek, Neve Campbell
- Long, dark hair and someone who's small and

petite with a nice body.

CLAIRE LIKES

- Ben Affleck
- 'Someone I can chat to, who makes me laugh and who's nice looking.'
- Men with dark hair and darkish skin.
- Handsome, funny, rich, successful men . . . like George Clooney!

THE FUTURE

So where exactly are Steps heading on their runaway fame train? That's a question no-one has an answer to. Lisa claims Steps are so busy they 'can't even look beyond next week – let alone next year!' Which isn't surprising considering the whirlwind year they've had. Already they've cut their second album, of which more is mentioned elsewhere, and promoting that is going to take them quite a long way into the next Millennium.

So what else can we expect from the fab five? A Steps movie would certainly be well worth seeing, but the boys and girls have some very firm views on that particular subject. 'We'd like to play characters, not just ourselves,' suggests Lee, while Faye favours something 'dead funky and way-out futuristic'.

Steps could doubtless put more into their performance than the Spice Girls did in *Spiceworld* – and judging by the response to the Disney medley in the current live show there would probably be a lot of dressing up involved. Who knows? The Osmonds and the Jackson Five had cartoons made in which their characters got up to all kinds of adventures, so maybe Steps will follow them (and H's favourite group,

Cleopatra) and become even more animated, if that's possible!

TV is a medium that's already been kind to Steps, so with Claire very much on the shortlist for a return to Ant and Dec's Saturday morning show, we could well see other Steps members making guest appearances elsewhere. Maybe we'll see H getting to grips with a 'make' on *Blue Peter*, while Lee would be right at home getting into sports-reporting mode with an item or two on *Football Focus*. He and Gary Lineker would get on like a house on fire – after all, Gary used to play for Everton once upon a time!

Faye and Lisa would be delighted to have the chance of doing some kind of dancercise vid, as both are keen on the dance-instruction side of things. In fact, you'll be seeing a snapshot of their abilities on a Steps long-form video, including the single clips and a lot more, that is scheduled for release in the near future. Lisa takes a dancing class, Claire passes on some of her home cooking tips – the new Delia Smith? The mind boggles! – and H shows how you too can become a circus clown!

With so many possibilities for where to go next, Lisa for one can't see anyone leaving the fold while things are going this well. But if the unthinkable ever did happen, she feels the pop world could benefit by having five stupendous solo performers instead of one great group. 'If we ever do split up then I'll definitely stay in the business. I'm sure most of us will – we're all entertainers.' Lisa can also see herself living in Australia '. . . when I'm grown-up! It's got such a cool vibe, the clubbing's brilliant and the place is beautiful.'

Assuming they stay on this side of the world, there are endless possibilities if Steps' members decided to carry on singing together. 'Me and Faye have decided to do a Danny and Sandy (from the *Grease* musical) tour if Steps split up,' joked Lee when one magazine had them dress up as the Travolta and Newton-John characters for a laugh. *Grease*, of course, finished its West End run this year after taking £6 million in ticket receipts, which leads us to another future possibility.

A stage musical starring Steps would be certain to be a sell-out success. They've all had experience on the boards, and if they each took a role with an equal share of the spotlight you'd have a show with all the spectacle of a pop concert. Who could possibly lose? You could take anything from *West Side Story* onwards and turn it into a box-office bonanza. It's a shame *Saturday Night Fever*'s already taken, because we know five people whose performance in it would be anything but a 'Tragedy' . . .

If ambitious Lee ever fancies going solo, he's got a ready-made role model in whose larger-than-life footsteps he can follow. 'I really admire Robbie Williams, purely for what he's done with his life. He started out the same way I have, in a pop band. Now he's gone one step further, justified the odds and proved a point. I'm not saying I want a solo career, but I admire the fact that he knows what he wants in life and has a positive head on his shoulders.'

Robbie is currently trying his darndest to break America with an album called *The Ego Has Landed*, combining the best bits of his first and second British efforts. It's a ploy the Backstreet Boys have also used with success. But whether or not Steps have to take one step backward to march two forward, it's certain the States will play a big part in their future. If they manage to become superstars there, they'll have beaten Abba and Take That, neither of whom really established themselves Stateside. So there's every incentive to follow Five and B*Witched as they make their name by constant touring and TV.

This, though, means basically dedicating a year out of your life to playing everywhere and anywhere in an effort to make friends and sell records. Along the way, you might be lucky enough to interest the Disney Channel or another satellite TV company in doing a special show on you. And that's only the beginning. If you do find success, you'll be expected to go round and do it all over again in bigger, better venues. Phew! Those Steps guys and gals are gonna need to be fit, fit, fit!

All of this means that, one way or another, we're going to see even less of Steps as their career progresses. Still, sharing them with the world is a small price to pay. And it means H, at least has no regrets about turning down a singing job on a cruise ship that he was offered the same day as Steps came calling. 'Everyone thought I was mad for not taking the cruise . . .' he smiles, but he got to see the world anyway! Best foot forward guys and here's to the future . . .

Are you ready to take

THE STEPS SUPERBRAIN CHALLENGE?

Have you kept in step with Steps . . . or are you several yards behind the group that sets the pace when it comes to pop? Find out the hard way as you struggle with these twenty-five testing questions! Select the appropriate answers, then compare them with our checklist – no cheating, now! Then add up the correct ones to find your final score.

1 Which Step has a pierced belly-button?
2 Which group first hit with 'Last Thing On My Mind'?
3 Which Step got a miniature motorbike as well as a baby sister?
4 What does Lisa collect from her air flights across the world?
5 Who walked Faye up the aisle in the 'Tragedy' video?
6 What does Lee have a collection of?
7 On which TV quiz programme did Faye fail to

shine?

8 Which Step appears on stage as a Red Indian Disney character?
9 Whose favourite impersonation is the Tasmanian Devil?
10 Which *Coronation Street* character is Faye always being mistaken for?
11 Which Step is named after a footballer?
12 How many hit singles came off *Step One*?
13 Whose nickname at school was 'Bear'?
14 Which footballer was Lisa's object of desire?
15 Which Step has sung with a member of the Honeyz?
16 Which plastic creature stolen from a seafood platter became Larry, Steps' mascot?
17 When H was a Redcoat, what did he have to dress up as?
18 Which ghost did Faye see running about in her garden?
19 Which Step was born on bonfire night?
20 Which Steps single was their first chart-topper?
21 How does H improve on nature, eye-wise?
22 What's the insect Faye hates . . . and H used to keep as a pet?
23 Which group beat *Step One* to the top of the album chart?
24 Where would Faye like her ideal birthday party to be?
25 In which country was '5,6,7,8' covered by a singer in a local language?

ANSWERS

1 Faye
2 Bananarama
3 Lee

4 Miniature drink bottles
5 Her dad
6 Silver jewellery
7 *Never Mind The Buzzcocks*
8 Faye
9 H
10 Hairdresser Maxine Heavey (alias actress Tracy Shaw)
11 Lee
12 Five
13 Claire
14 David Beckham
15 Claire
16 A lobster
17 A scarecrow
18 The ghost of her dog
19 Lisa
20 'Heartbeat'/'Tragedy'
21 He wears coloured contacts
22 A spider
23 Manic Street Preachers
24 Hawaii
25 Malaysia

HOW DID YOU DO?

0–6

Oh dear – time you got in Step! There's a lot you've (better best) forgotten, or maybe didn't even know, so get your Steps collection out and enjoy a treasure hunt!

7–12

That's better – but like Faye's hair extensions you're hanging on for dear life. There's more to Steps than meets the eye – as you can find out if you try. It's fun, too . . .

13–18
This is good stuff – you know what's happening, and there's not far to go before you're a Steps superbrain. Keep it up and you'll soon be Number 1, just like a group we know!

19–25
Okay, which of you is it? Lee, Faye, Lisa, H or Claire? Congratulations, you're a Steps superbrain if ever we saw one! Now start on the dance moves . . .